Finding Intimacy in a Love-Starved World

Radical Truth for Singles

Cindy Janczyk

FINDING INTIMACY IN A LOVE-STARVED WORLD
Copyright © 2007 Cindy Janczyk

ISBN 978-1-886068-30-8
Library of Congress Control Number: 2007934147
Personal Growth · Christian Life

Published by Fruitbearer Publishing
P.O. Box 777, Georgetown, DE 19947 · (302) 856-6649 · FAX (302) 856-7742
www.fruitbearer.com • fruitbearer.publishing@verizon.net
Graphic design by Candy Abbott; cover photo from shutterstock.com
Edited by Fran Lowe and Marjorie Vawter

All Scripture quotations, unless otherwise indicated, are taken from the HOLY BIBLE, NEW INTER-NATIONAL VERSION®, NIV®, Copyright © 1973, 1978, 1984 International Bible Society. Used by permission of Zondervan Bible Publishers. All rights reserved.

Scripture quotations marked KJV are taken from the The King James Version of the Holy Bible (KJV), public domain.

All rights reserved. No part of this publication may be reproduced, stored in a retrieval system, or transmitted in any form or by any means—electronic, mechanical, photocopy, recording, or any other—except for brief quotations in printed reviews, without the prior permission of the publisher or author, except as provided by USA copyright law.

Printed in the United States of America

Dedicated

to

Gettysburg Master's Commission

Dan, Christa, Shannon, Ashley, all the students . . .
without you I never would have started typing.

Table of Contents

Foreword 9
1. The Canyon of Love Failure 11
2. Everyone Is Crying for Intimacy 17
3. All You Need Is . . . Intimacy 21

Part 1—DIVINE INTIMACY 25
4. The Greatest Commandment 27
5. God Loves Loving *Me?* 31
6. Did Anybody Tell You "I Love You" Today? 35
7. Jesus, Lover of My Soul? 39
8. It's Not About Becoming Female 43
9. Where the Longing Is Finally Satisfied 47
10. Till Death Do Us Part 51
11. Focused Passion 55
12. A Little Parable with a Big Message 59
13. I Want to Know You the Way You Want To Be Known 63
14. Who Is God, Anyway? 67
15. So How Do You Relate to an Invisible God? 71
16. God Wants to Talk with You 75
17. Winning the Battle of Unbelief 81

Table of Contents, cont.

Part 2—HUMAN INTIMACY 85
   18. The Way We Were 89
   19. The Way We Are 95
   20. How the Curse Affected Women 99
   21. How the Curse Affected Men 105
   22. Love Is Sex—True or False? 111
   23. What's So Bad about Sin, Anyway? 117
   24. Promiscuity . . . I Want To Be Accepted 123
   25. Cohabitation . . . I Want To Be Sure 127
   26. Homosexuality . . . I Want To Be Real 133
   27. Do You Really Want To Be Free? 137
   28. Shame Is the Thief of Intimacy 143
   29. Dating with a Purpose 149
   30. Dating Boundaries 153
   31. Finding Mr./Ms. Right 159
   32. Intimacy Is God's Plan for Love 163

Endnotes 169
About the Author 173
To Order This Book 175

Foreword

Our marriage didn't start off on the right foot. Whereas ministry and public leadership came very easy to us, we realized on our honeymoon that a healthy marriage was going to take a lot of hard work. A few months into our marriage, we decided to get serious about health and the first person we looked to was Cindy. It was during those months of meeting with Cindy and her husband, Hank, that we realized her unique gift of teaching on the essence of healthy relationships, whether you are married or single. After sitting under her teaching, we realized that the college students in the ministry we were leading needed to hear this as well.

What you are about to read is the result of years of teaching college students not only how to have healthy relationships, but how to discover the DNA of healthy relationships. When we first asked Cindy to teach our students, we explicitly asked her not to just create another "how-to" manual. If you were to go to your local bookstore, you would find a lot of books telling you how to do relationships, but very few if any that reveal the DNA of relationships. This book is not just a relationship book. It is a theology book. In these pages, you will discover the essence of all your relationships, that over arching principle that can make or break them. This DNA is seen throughout Scripture. It was the foundation of Adam's relationship with Eve, the thesis of the Song of Solomon, the motivating factor of Christ's ministry, the coming fulfillment of His promise to return... and the center of your connection to others. The great thing is that this DNA already resides inside of all of us. What is it? It is God's unstoppable quest to reconnect with humanity and our struggle to know our Maker. Simply put, when our connection with God is at the center of our relationships, we find life fulfilling and thrilling.

Our prayer as you read this book is that you will discover the adventure found in each of your relationships. Enjoy the ride.

Dan and Christa Hubbell
Founders of Gettysburg Master's Commission
Pastors of University Church, Philadelphia

Chapter 1

The Canyon of Love Failure

You're in your twenty-somethings, and I'm in my forty-somethings. We're standing on two opposite sides of a vast canyon, gazing at the people below. They represent hundreds of thousands of hurting relationships—Cupid's casualties. Each one began with high hopes of lasting romance, but somehow love failed. One couple is divorced after forty years of marriage; another is divorced after forty days of marriage. Two lovers are separated after three years of living together; another pair is separated after one romantic evening. The range of relationship scenarios that end up in the Canyon of Failed Love are too many to count.

Having finished your journey through childhood, you've just arrived at a new decade. It's a thrilling time of life when most choose a marriage partner and a career field, but the road of promise has taken you to the edge of this canyon scene. From where I stand, I can see the anticipation of a bright future draining from your countenance. Predictions overpower optimism with the terrifying reality that your love life will also end up in this pit. Sarcasm hides the face of discouragement: "If this is the inevitable, I'll just blow off the world! It's all about living for myself and hoping for the best anyway."

But the voice of wishful thinking offers no guarantees, and the questions still pulsate throughout your being: "Is there any way around the pain of failed love relationships? Does marriage still work?" Looking back over your shoulder, there sure isn't much in your childhood experience that would give you reason to hope, is there?

My generation has defined marriage as a loose commitment with many back doors. Why would anyone in your generation find marriage inviting? Most of you have experienced the pain of divorce up close and personal. You've lived in homes full of deceit, anger, discord, control, and false love. When you were kids, many of your parents made the decision to get a divorce. Whether it was justified or careless, divorce was far from the most desirable solution in your world. Torn in two by divided affections and loyalties, your private pain was diminished by the growing numbers of children who shared your agonizing experience. Most kids your age were forced to adapt to the inconvenience of separate holidays, alternating weekend schedules, and "move over" readjustment demands that came with a new step family. The "get over it" expectation is often fed by the myth of childhood resilience, but that kind of pain just isn't a simple hurdle to overcome.

The failure of countless marriages, however, is certainly not limited to divorce court. For the first twenty years of your life, you were indoctrinated with messages from the entertainment world that laughed in the face of traditional marriage. Sitcoms portrayed married love as boring and fickle. Romance movies slavishly followed the formula of the innocuous love-triangle featuring an adulterous heroine whose "love" relationship appeared far more genuine and attractive than that of her married partner.

Sadly, the movie industry became the bible for my generation and, without hesitation, we followed their lead and engaged in the relationship models they offered. Satisfaction within relationships became synonymous with sex, and the ultimate experience could only be found in the thrilling challenge of secret adultery. Both men and women married their careers and barely tolerated their families. Marriage became a display case of fake faces looking pretty and acting happy for formal occasions with a temporary show of tradition. After the weddings and funerals were over, the superficial exchange of shallow affection continued with sickening repetition. Without a doubt, these marriages are also represented in the Canyon of Failed Love.

I watch you sigh a second time as the cultural norms of marriage avoidance begin to make a lot of sense. You've seen so few marriages with any appeal that you're skeptical about the entire institution. When you make the rare discovery of a great marriage, it's easy to conclude that the strength of their love lies in a mysterious destiny of luck. "They were just meant for each other," you reason. Without a little magic, the prospects of repeating the cycle of love failure looks unavoidable. Is marriage outdated? Does anyone take wedding vows seriously anymore? Is it possible to stay in love for a lifetime?

Your generation has tried to find alternative routes around the Canyon of Failed Love. Who wouldn't? Out of sheer desperation to avoid the inevitable, most of you have concluded that marriage is a thing of the past. Your prevention plan for failure is to simply bypass the wedding! Your philosophy is that if you're not married, you can't be divorced. Consequently, cohabitation has become the norm of romance with a mass of followers believing relationship without commitment is the smart way to go.

Since "true love" is still characterized by sex, the appeal for sexual variety is becoming the new trend, with same-sex partners seeking to redefine marriage as we've known it. Of course, these couples are motivated by a desire for successful relationships, but the innovative plan of tolerance doesn't come with any guarantees. These couples also end up in the Canyon of Failed Love with gaping wounds caused by rejection, abuse, and a never-ending sense of doubt that romance is anything more than a fantasy. I watch your sigh turn into a look of confusion—then panic. You turn to run, but there is no other path. There is no way around this canyon! You must walk straight ahead. "Okay, okay," you say. "If I must go forward, is it possible to learn from their mistakes and discover a love that really works?"

"Yes! Yes! Yes!" I shout from the other side of the canyon. Can you hear my cry of hope? Love *does* work, in the arms of a marriage that follows God's plan, and it is awesome! There is *nothing* better than the romance of married love. I am someone who has a satisfying love relationship with the first man I married, and I am among many who share this testimony. We are on the other side of the canyon, cheering you on with confidence. It's not a hope based on luck, faith in love, or even great chemistry. No, my marriage almost failed after twelve years of genuine effort. Our hope is based on the truth of God's plan for successful love. God designed marriage, and the reason it has worked in the past is the exact reason it still works today—God is faithful. When we follow His plan for married love, we will find the alternative to love failure.

I want to build a bridge of hope between the two of us. Will you give me that opportunity? I've taken many notes on relationships since my twenty-somethings. I don't have all the answers, but I'm eager to share what I've learned with you. I can't promise you that the journey of love will be painless, but I can offer you the hope that true love is really attainable. You don't want to end up on the casualty list of marriage failures, so you'll need a bridge of guidance to help you find success. Love comes along a path of discovery that includes some rather unconventional methods of thinking. God is the God of passion and inconsolable longing. There's no one better to learn it from, but you'll have to get to know God as a romantic before you can comprehend the meaning of true love between a man and woman.

You'll have to trust me as I present radical truth that is seldom taught today. Although our culture has just about abandoned the Holy Bible as a relic of the past, God's Word remains timeless. He is speaking a specific message of hope to your generation through the Song of Solomon, and it's strikingly relevant for our day. God cares about your generation, dear one, and He longs to establish a lasting legacy of His love through your relationships. You are the remnant generation, a people set apart for a holy passion.

One last thing before we continue. On behalf of my generation, I want to say, "I'm truly sorry." These words do not begin to embrace the chasm of remorse I feel because of the prevailing falsehood and confusion that we have modeled for you in marriage. I want to recognize our contribution to your negative view of traditional marriage.

There are many reasons for divorce. Some are clearly understandable, but most are not. Without dismissing the pain of the struggles encountered in marriage, I can truly say that most people who marry are unprepared for how much work it takes to make it great. That has been, in my opinion, where we have failed you the most; so many of us entered marriage with little more confidence than a slim hope for the best. We did not understand the wisdom of mate selection, the basics of married living, and the role God desired to play in our relationships. Had we known and heeded these biblical principles, I think we could have avoided the reputation of failure.

What's done is done, but the one resolution I have made is to share the message of truth with you. Knowing our shameful track record, I'm determined to give back what I've learned. I have faith that your generation can rise above the current social trends with convincing proof that God's design in marriage offers a contagious love that still works. When you succeed, many will follow.

Chapter 2
Everyone is Crying for Intimacy

Intimacy. Everyone craves it, but few know where to find it. It's the underlying motivation for men caught in the addictive ring of pornography. It's behind the emotional vacuum of pro-abortion activists handing out condoms. It's the heart cry of a teenage girl settling for promiscuous relationships. It's the desperation of a schoolboy using weapons to release pain.

Intimacy is a critical human need, but it's such a foreign concept that we're easily persuaded by cheap substitutes. Pressed by newspaper and TV advertising to believe that real intimacy is found in the lingerie department, instant pleasure can be purchased on a credit card. But it's void of meaning, totally worthless. The reruns are getting boring; the same old sex scenes cannot satisfy the thirst for belonging and acceptance. We're starved for worth, but we're caught in a game of hide-and-seek without any clue of what to look for. Intimacy was never meant to be so evasive.

Most of us got our first idea of what love *should be* from Disney. Those romantic images of Cinderella and the prince still carry with them a standard of ideal love in the minds of Americans. Whether you're male or female, there's a distinct fascination with human attraction. Embedded in our DNA is a quality of humanness that searches for depth in our relationships. Daughters dream of their wedding day while sons live to win the heart of a beautiful girl. This fascination is not a sex drive, but a need for intimacy. God gave every human being an innate desire to be loved unconditionally in the arms of one individual for life. Yes, intimacy is the essence of true love and this missing piece can still to be found.

> *"Teacher, which is the greatest commandment in the Law?" Jesus replied, "'Love the Lord your God with all your heart and with all your soul and with all your mind.' This is the first and greatest commandment. And the second is like it: 'Love your neighbor as yourself.'"*
>
> Matthew 22:36–39

Jesus used these two commandments to make an important point about forming successful relationships. He was saying that in order to understand the benefits of human love, your primary attention needs to be on a love relationship with God. Most of us spend a lot more energy on the second commandment. "Loving your neighbor" feels a lot more tangible, and it usually includes some measure of charity or sacrifice. But notice that Jesus did not list it as the ultimate commandment. Love for people is obviously important but our priorities are upside-down. Jesus is calling us to reexamine the meaning of our relationship with God—to experience His love so we are able to love others. If you're ever going to find the alternative route through the Canyon of Failed Love, you need to understand the importance of the first commandment and how it works. This is where relationship success begins.

What's Unconditional Love Really Feel Like?

Taking time to consider what He's about and who He really is will lead you down a path of incredible satisfaction. But most of all, you will learn that He is fully and totally consumed with love for you. You see, when you take the time to love the Lord with everything that is in you, you eventually discover that He loves you—emphatically! He enjoys you, He cares about you, and He is always talking about you—you're *always* on His mind! You cannot build a relationship with God without the topic of "you" coming up in the discussion. In fact, He *rarely* changes the subject.

When you make the first commandment your pursuit in life, you cannot avoid the surprising realization that God is absolutely crazy about you. And you just can't get to know Him without adopting that love for yourself. Loving God includes loving what He loves: *you!* It's not a cocky, arrogance that pushes people away but a gradual appreciation for who God designed you to be. Your version of humanity does not come with a copy; there is only one you throughout the entire span of time! He's proud of His design, and He wants to show you off like a proud parent. But most of all, He wants you to recognize how awesome you are. This is unconditional love.

Without love for yourself, you'll never be able to follow the second commandment. *"Love your neighbor as yourself"* or "Love people to the extent that you love yourself." Most people do not even *like* themselves, let alone *love* themselves. It's a universal problem that escalates into war. We *need* to know we're loved, and we are desperate to know we're lovable! Apart from a love for yourself there is no love to give. The Canyon of Love Failure is full of people in search of intimacy, but they have no idea that the real missing piece isn't love from without but love from within.

Chapter 3
All You Need Is . . . Intimacy

Their relationship began in 1995. Tanya Nicole Kach was an eighth grader who met Thomas Hose, a security officer in his thirties, at school. After many secret meetings on the school stairwell and hushed phone conversations, they "fell in love." Soon, they devised a plan for her to move in with him.

Tanya ran away from home at age fourteen to go live with Thomas. Their home consisted of a small two-story house where Tanya was confined to a tiny bedroom. In exchange for sex, she was given food, secondhand clothes, and a bucket to use as a bathroom. Her horrible living conditions lasted ten years.

In 2005, Hose found a way to change Tanya's identity to Nikki Allen so she could go outside for short periods of time during the day. It was then that Tanya began to realize her living situation was abnormal. Later, she confessed, "I was scared—I came to realize that other people's relationships weren't like that."[1]

The story hit the newspapers and national networks in March of 2006, when Tanya managed to communicate to a grocery clerk her desire to leave Koch. The Associated Press release ran side-by-side a front-page photo of a beautiful blonde with model-like features cradled in her daddy's arms. Although her bizarre relationship with Koch was a picture of obvious dysfunction, who could argue that at one time this wasn't true love? For ten years, Tanya had been convinced.

In our society, love has many definitions; people are free to make it what they want it to be. Cohabitation, same-sex marriage, and even polygamy are the latest relationship trends, all falling under the heading of "love." Every one of these living arrangements, however, points to the dramatic shift away from the concept of traditional marriage. The fact of the matter is we live in a society that has been experiencing massive relationship failure for the past twenty-five years, and the pain of these breakups has forced us to choose alternatives out of sheer desperation. Most young adults have been either raised in a home with a divorced single parent, a stepparent, or two unmarried partners. Because they have witnessed firsthand the result of failed marriage relationships, a predominant percentage of them are now abandoning marriage altogether, reasoning that it is an old-fashioned institution that just doesn't work anymore.

Cohabitation has become a cultural norm, with many people viewing it as a prevention plan for failed marriages. For them, "living together" is a litmus test to confirm compatibility. Despite its lousy track record for ensuring successful marriages, cohabitation entices singles with the perks of sexual freedom and tax benefits, encouraging them to continue under the pretense of love. Since love has become equated with sex, there is now an escalating drive for sexual variety. The ultimate love experience is no longer limited to heterosexual relations, so the perversion line has been blurred. We are in desperate need for the reconstruction of love's truest definition; what we *really* need is intimacy.

Intimacy Begins With Jesus

If you really want to find intimacy in a love-starved world, you need to begin with the One who designed the concept: God. He has what the world longs for because He is the only one who understands how intimacy really works. The strength of human love hinges on this love source. Jesus is the only one who can love without a single condition. He qualified as the best one to handle your heart when He proved His love on the cross. No one's ever gone that far for you! Satan offers convincing counterfeits in all sorts of packages because he knows God's love is revolutionary. Once you get this message, it will change your life! Make no mistake, God intended for your love needs to be fully and completely met through an intimate relationship with Jesus Christ. Herein lies the key to intimacy in the twenty-first century.

The Power of Intimacy

God longs to restore His identity as the Lover of your soul, for your own personal benefit, but there's more to it than that. Intimacy brings new meaning to the Bible's message. When I begin to *really* believe that God loves me, and you begin to *really* believe that God loves you, there is a growing number of "believers" who are enjoying the love of God on a daily basis. Inevitably, we start to live as people who are loved, and it totally changes our outlook and our responses. Eventually, people start to notice. John 17:23 says, *"I in them and you in me. May they be brought to complete unity to let the world know that you sent me and have loved them even as you have loved me."* His love is contagious!

Jesus Christ is returning someday, but before He does, God is looking for those who will pursue a personal, passionate love relationship with His Son. Once you understand that developing an intimate relationship with Christ comes first, you will be better equipped to understand what it takes to *"love your neighbor as yourself."* The manifestation of human intimacy comes to men and women as a result of this vital bond with Christ. Human intimacy is never more beautiful or satisfying than it is with a married couple in love with Jesus.

Part 1

Divine Intimacy

Jesus replied,
"'Love the Lord your God with all your heart
and with all your soul and with all your mind.'
This is the first and greatest commandment.
And the second is like it: 'Love your neighbor as yourself.'"

MATTHEW 22:37–39

Chapter 4

The Greatest Commandment

Jesus knew how much the disciples wanted to please Him, so He explained it in simple terms. What was most important to Him had far more to do with relationship than law. Jesus was saying, "Hey, guys, I know what the law says, but let Me give you the shortened version. Just get to know Me, and you'll become familiar with My love. That's right, just put all your energy, time, and attention into learning about My love for you. I want that more than anything! And guess what? While you're learning about My love for you, you'll start to feel love for people around you. In fact, when you come to believe My love for you is real, than you'll overflow with love for others, even those people who are hard to get along with. That's how the law works."

Since Jesus walked this earth, not much has changed with our perception of what God expects from us. Oh, we don't make animal sacrifices to atone for our sin, but we do have a full lineup of religious "requirements" that we think God expects of us. Going to church, reading the Bible regularly, praying for the needs of others, giving tithes and offerings, taking communion, going to confession, just to name a few. But God wants more from us than just obedience; what really warms His heart is our relationship with Him.

Jesus has this burning passion to know you intimately. It's a feeling that He also placed within you when He designed you. He wants you to fall in love with Him! It's not so much about following the rules as it is discovering the reality of God's love. This is the motivation that prompts you to obey Him in every area of life.

You Gotta Love Yourself in Order to Love Others

The first and greatest commandment is to love God with everything that is in you. This is where intimacy begins. His instruction not only conveys the seriousness of honoring Him but it also categorizes a relationship with Jesus as a top priority, #1 by far. Only in this order will you gain the love for human relationships. When Jesus becomes your primary love source you can access essential ingredients for building successful relationships *with people.* Remember the little tag Jesus put on the verse? *"And the second one is like it: Love your neighbor as yourself."* Yes, Jesus is instructing us to love our neighbors to the same extent that we love ourselves, but this is far more profound than a simple call to be thoughtful.

Most people do not love themselves. When we really think about it, we are our own worst critics. When we look in the mirror, we do not mimic Gaston, the arrogant suitor in the Disney movie *Beauty and the Beast.* On the contrary, we know where all our flaws exist, so we work very hard to conceal them. If they're not superficial imperfections, they're character flaws or those sins from our past that chain us to a destiny of regret. Sadly, the degree of hate that has spread across the earth is indicative of the love*lessness* that most people have for themselves. We don't *love* ourselves, so we can't *love* our neighbors, either.

However, when your focus becomes the love of God, developing a love for yourself is inevitable. You cannot fall in love with Jesus without starting to love who He loves—you! When you love the Lord with all your heart, soul, and mind, something changes on the inside. His love for you is so extraordinary that you just can't help noticing who He loves the most. This is a God who enjoys you and wants to hang out with you. This is a God who thinks you're awesome and wants everyone to know it! You just can't hear too much of that love talk without starting to believe it. As amazing as it sounds, growing in the knowledge of God's love for you makes love for your neighbor come naturally.

God's Love Makes You Attractive

There is one more benefit to loving the Lord with all your heart, soul, and mind. God wants you to have a very satisfying love life. He knows that when you fall in love with Him, your countenance will change. There is a striking confidence that accompanies divine intimacy; there's really nothing on earth to compare it to. It's more than a good self-image or an inner peace that comes with accepting your strengths and weaknesses. God's love makes you impressive! You know you're loved with an unconditional love that will never end, and it shows in how you carry yourself. In fact, this countenance makes you very attractive to the opposite sex! It's God's way of playing matchmaker. When two people find their significance, purpose, and need for belonging in Jesus, they give God the control to orchestrate their entire love life. He doesn't miss a single detail of romance in His plan, which far exceeds anything Hollywood could ever portray on film.

Chapter 5

God Loves Loving *Me?*

Relationships define us as human. No other species on the planet relates to one another in quite the same way because we are the only ones who can think and form opinions. We have personal preferences, views, and convictions that distinguish us from any other species. A rhino never takes time to think about the AIDS epidemic in Africa or even why his water hole is empty. It was not created to have an opinion. We have thoughts and feelings that define who we are and help us establish values to live by. That's because humans were designed to look and feel like God. The Bible says, we were created *in the image of God*. Cool. That makes human beings exceedingly special. Like you, God has a personality. He has strong preferences, views, and convictions, particularly about you. In fact, the thrust of His emotional makeup is centered on desiring a relationship with *you*. But few of us understand the depth of His desire.

Relating to God's Love in a New Way

I was blessed to be born and raised in a home with two loving parents. Living in the inner city of Baltimore, Daddy made just enough to keep us in the low end of middle class, but I never felt lack. Love was consistent. We had a routine of going to church every week, and I have vivid memories of going to Sunday school, learning about the

Bible and God's love for me. (I know it sounds squeaky clean, but hey, that was my childhood experience.) I followed the teacher's "Repeat after me . . ." prayers of confession that led to an invitation of Jesus into my heart. (I always prayed them, just in case Jesus didn't hear me the last time.) At age twelve, I attended a summer camp where I heard sermons every night. I had heard the Easter story so many times, but suddenly it made sense on a *personal* level. Christ died for *me*. He was more than a historical figure. Somehow, the reality of His love demonstrated on the cross touched my heart, and I knew it was truth. Without hesitation, I walked down the aisle as a public profession of my faith. I wanted to live my life in gratitude for His sacrifice. Taking my commitment very seriously, I started rearranging the priorities of my life. I started reading the Bible, trying to understand it, and I talked to God, imagining Him as a friend—sort of like a grandfather. I don't know if we were close, but God was really important to me. I worked at including Him in my life. He was there to listen and give advice, but I never really considered that God wanted to share His heart with me.

Several years ago, I attended a worship conference that changed my life. There were many speakers representing ministries from all across the United States. Without any cooperative effort between them, God placed a message on each of their hearts that carried the common theme of Christ, the Bridegroom. It was obvious that God had something to say, and without question, He wanted to be identified by this personal, intimate title.

During my whole upbringing I had never heard any teaching on intimacy with Jesus. I understood that Jesus wanted to be my personal Lord and Savior, but my relationship with God was never described in intimate terms. At this conference, however, I was captivated by the subject. Like a child after her first taste of ice cream, I wanted more.

I'll never forget the keynote speaker's sermon from the book of Esther. Through this biblical story, he was able to explain the mysterious love of Christ in a way I could finally grasp. There was such a strong feeling of romance in the room. At the end, he gave an altar call, inviting those in the audience who had never experienced intimate love with God to come forward. We were sitting in a large auditorium full of pastors, worship leaders, and their team members, yet when the call went out, only a few people remained seated. Crowds of men and women flooded the altar, the stage, and the aisles. Each person sobbed tears of revelation. I was among them.

I had walked with God for so many years, yet I had never known this kind of love. I felt like I was meeting Jesus for the very first time. In a private moment at the altar, I heard Him say to me, "I know you love me, Cindy. I have watched you serve Me with faithfulness and great devotion for many years, but you have not fully believed in My love for you." Even though I couldn't see Him in a physical form, I knew He was looking into my face with tears brimming in His eyes. Revelation flooded my soul, and I realized then I had spent so much energy trying to prove my love for Him that I had never thought about His desire to give love to me.

It is a frustrating experience when love is offered but not received. We can accept the reality of God's love without embracing it, personally. Somehow, in that brief moment, I was able to feel His anguish. I vowed that day to live my life with a different focus. From then on, I wanted Him to have the satisfaction that His love was getting through and that all He had done to prove His love was worth the effort. Yes, He demonstrated His love by dying on the cross, but this God of love didn't stop there. Christ was inviting me to journey with Him through a daily relationship characterized by endless love experiences. Every day would be a new discovery of how God enjoys me. The cement was still wet—the fact that God loved, loving me was not quite a truth I could stand on, but I was drinking in the potential of that thought. This was a totally new message. God wasn't finished loving me. Wow! I vowed to live life just to give Him the satisfaction that His love was working.

Chapter 6

Did Anybody Tell You "I Love You" Today?

What comes to mind when you hear someone say, "I love you"? Think about it. Do you register "I love the way you make me feel"? Maybe those three words come with expectations like "You better give me something in return," or it is temporary. "I love you today, but tomorrow is still questionable." Does "I love you" mean "I want to have sex with you"? Have you ever heard "I enjoy being with you . . . period"?

When our children were little they attended a local preschool. They would sing a song that I'll never forget. "Did anybody tell you 'I love you' today? Did anybody tell you 'I love you' today? Did anybody tell you 'I love you' today? Let me be the first. Put me on your list. I love you, today." I was always looking for another way to state this term of endearment so I adopted this song. I would sing this on a regular basis, and it communicated such warmth and acceptance. They would voluntarily climb up on my lap just to get closer to the message. It felt so good to love and to be loved in return. Then I would say. "I'm so glad God gave you to me, but you know what? If you were standing in a long line of children and God had given me the option to choose any one of them to come live in our family, I would have still picked you!"

Everyone wants to belong. It's an emotional place of stability where love is offered without one single condition. You are loved simply because you are you. Belonging is a secure place of guaranteed love that no one else shares. You don't ever have to fight to gain it or maintain it. When you belong, you have the assurance of a place that will never be altered by your mistakes or your failures. You are in, and you never have to fear rejection or abandonment. It is a wonderful place. Everyone *needs* to belong because that's the way we were designed.

Sadly, there are a lot of people in this world who have no idea what the emotion feels like. Singles bars and college campuses are full of children walking around in adult bodies, still searching for a place of acceptance. For whatever reason, the love message didn't get through, so they live life with gaping holes in their security system. Unaware of their lack, they pretend to have it all together. Following the current of social norms, they adapt to what is acceptable, disguising the intense desire to be wanted. But they just can't find anything to replace the missing piece. They long to belong.

A friend of mine really struggled with this. She had been adopted by two loving parents, but for some reason she continually agonized over her true identity. "Who are my real parents, and where are they now?" "Why did they put me up for adoption?" "Do they think of me and would they like to meet me?" The questions tormented her. She could not resolve the feeling of rejection, but the truth terrified her. What if her parents didn't miss her? What if they had no interest in seeing their baby girl? She was never able to get past the unknown. How desperate she was for answers, but she could never get past her fears. In fact, the unknown kept her from ever bonding with her adoptive parents whose love was sure. Belonging is a gift.

Do you realize that you can belong to God? No matter where you've been or what you've done, He is eager to call you His own. Just listen to what He has to say about you.

> *"I took you from the ends of the earth, from its farthest corners I called you. I said, 'You are my servant.' I have chosen you and have not rejected you."*
>
> Isaiah 41:9

God the Father loves you! God the Father wants you! When you're standing in that long line of kids, He points to you and says, "That one over there. Yep, that's the one I pick." Everyone should know what it's like to feel chosen. There's no place like it.

Unfortunately, parents mess up. I don't know your circumstances, but I'm sure that your mom or dad failed to love you somewhere along the way. I'm not excusing their behavior, but you don't have to let it define you either. There were plenty of times I blew it too. I had to say I'm sorry, *a lot!* But forgiveness makes it possible to move on from the mistake and the pain. The agony of neglect and rejection will never subside until you choose to forgive.

The truth is, perfect parents were never part of the plan. They were once kids too, with similar challenges of incomplete love. God the Father is the ultimate parent. He is the only dependable source of love. He will sing, *"Did anybody tell you 'I love you' today?—*and tomorrow and forever?" You bring Him excessive joy, and He'll never grow weary of repeating the phrase. In fact, because He loves you so much, He was willing to send His Son to show that love to you. God is in heaven, but Jesus came to earth where we could see Him, touch Him, and really begin to understand His love. Jesus made it possible for you and me to have relationship with God. He died for you. No one else has gone that far to prove their love.

Jesus understands your need, and He stands ready to meet it. In fact, the more desperate you are, the better positioned you are to receive the fullest measure of His infinite love. A relationship with God begins with a simple request. "God, I want to know you." If you really mean it, this prayer will change your life.

Chapter 7

Jesus, Lover of My Soul?

Do you realize that someone wants you? Do you know that someone is pursuing you? That's right. The search is over. You are everything they hoped for and now they feel complete. Want to know who's on the other side of the room, waiting for you? Jesus Christ, your ultimate Lover.

From Genesis to Revelation, the Bible is a love letter from God to His church, but it isn't merely a "Smile, God loves you" kind of love. This is a passionate love that is so strong and mysterious that most of the church avoids the subject altogether. We spend a lot of time studying and teaching on virtually every other personality of Christ, but few know Him as the Bridegroom. That kind of love is hard to grasp, especially when you've never heard it taught. How can God, who is perfect and holy, love you like a bridegroom loves his bride? For those who dare to take a closer look at this title God gave His Son, there is endless satisfaction. It's an ocean of intrigue waiting to be discovered, and eternity will not even bring you close to the finish line.

The Bible uses wedding analogies to describe the *type* of love God offers and the intentions He has for a future kingdom: Jesus Christ, the King of Kings and Lord of Lord, will marry His bride, the church—those who eagerly submit to His authority and who actively pursue intimacy with the Savior. The book literally opens and closes with magnificent wedding scenes, giving us more than a clue to the pivotal emphasis God places on this specific quality of love. At the end of the age, the Spirit and the bride will cry, *"Come, Lord Jesus!"* (see Revelation 22:17). Pulsating with a rhythmic chorus, this anthem is already being sung across the earth with increasing passion and volume.

But many are still scratching their heads over the concept. "I just don't get it," is a common response to this teaching—especially among forty-somethings or older. In fact, designating Jesus as the Bridegroom is almost offensive because it sounds so . . . well . . . out there.

I am not advocating imbalance, a fixation on one personality, minimizing all the other characteristics of Christ. But there is a desperate need to identify with this personality in this generation. The world is starved for love and Jesus, as the Bridegroom offers a unique relationship based on intimacy that is not portrayed in any other identity.

Every title of God is meaningful, but all of them include plural followers: a shepherd has many sheep, a warrior has many soldiers, a king has many subjects. *But a bridegroom only has ONE bride!*

Think about it. Everything about falling in love involves exclusive love. There is no competition, no doubt, and no interruption to experiential love. The Bridegroom extends love with such a wholehearted passion that it leaves you feeling like you're the only one He's ever loved. This is precisely the type of relationship God desires with you. It is God's way of saying, "I want to have a relationship that's defined by intimacy."

This is what it's like to know God. This passionate relationship of constant devotion is called divine intimacy. It's where you belong, and it's never too late to begin the journey.

Help Me Understand This, Lord

When I first started learning about this unique title of Christ, I remember asking God to help me grasp the concept. Even though I knew that I was a part of the Bride of Christ, it was a stretch for me to comprehend Jesus' desire for intimacy with me. I recognized that this was something very special, but I still couldn't get excited about it. I just kept visualizing this mental picture of a very long line of Christians waiting to see the Bridegroom like Santa in a mall display. No one wants to share their Lover!

One particular night, the sky had a rich, blue-black color that almost looked like velvet. The stars were very bright, but the moon had a shine that boasted of God's glory. It was spectacular! As I gazed into the galaxy, I heard His voice ask me, "Do you like it?" I was stunned by His question. The Almighty God of the universe was asking *me* if I liked His moon. Why should He care what I think? He's God!

In that moment, I connected with the Bridegroom who not only cares about what I think, but also lives to make me smile. The moon is one of my favorite parts of creation—it's definitely in my "Top Five." That night, I suddenly realized that He made it for me. You don't have to believe it, but I know He did. Maybe He made a waterfall or a sunset for you. Perhaps the deer in the backwoods or the trout in a lake were created with you in mind. At any rate, God is completely fascinated by what brings you pleasure. He's constantly looking for ways to communicate His love to you. I don't understand how Jesus can have an intimate relationship with each one of us, but I do know that I never feel like I have to share Him. He has the ability to be everything for every member of His Bride, and the sensation of connecting with His passionate love is beyond awesome. This is where true intimacy begins.

Chapter 8

It's Not About Becoming Female

"You're going to marry a man who is rugged." God spoke this into my heart when I was teenager and that is, indeed, a perfect description of my husband. His athletic background developed muscular strength and endurance in his body. Despite arthritis, surgical scars, and a posture with a near-permanent bend at the hips, past memories of the tackles and touchdowns still produce a chuckle from his gut. He's never been distracted by sweat, spit, or dirt under his fingernails (even though he usually bites them off before dirt has time to collect), and he still has the grit-your-teeth passion for life. He is a man's man whose battle scars and gray hair make him even more attractive as he ages.

My husband is a faithful finisher, a tremendous provider, and a caring father. Best of all, I love the unique blend of this rugged man who is also a passionate, sensitive lover of Jesus. It sweeps me off my feet whenever I see his large frame kneel at the altar in prayer or when he raises his hands in praise to his wonderful Savior. Those are the times when I witness the countenance of the Bride of Christ shining through the image of a man. It is truly inspirational to see.

God Loves Your Masculinity

Men, to be a member of the Bride of Christ does *not* mean that you are any less manly. It simply means that you are more humble. God *loves* your masculinity and identifies with your inner instinct for war and zeal for victory. To be the Bride of Christ means so much more than looking beautiful for the wedding. No, we are desperate for a warrior bride who can stand and fight the good fight with valor. Whether you're a mechanic, a farmer, a broker, or a coach, the battlefield is in your blood because God put it there. To be known as His Bride takes you beyond the role of a helpful servant to the noble cause of a mighty warrior conquering the armies of darkness to bring forth the kingdom of light. Men of God, join the ranks of those empowered by a consuming passion for Christ and the advancement of His kingdom. Oh, how the feminine side of the Bride *needs* the masculine side in order to win the battle of the ages.

We Can't Do This Without You

Typically, men really struggle with the notion that they are members of the Bride of Christ. The sexual implications are just too distracting for them to see the beauty of relational intimacy. In fact, many Christian men are fooled into thinking that their need for approval can only be found in sexual fantasy, but Jesus is the only true answer to their desperate cry for self-worth. Come on, men, the Bridegroom concept did not originate around the table of a ladies' tea party! God Almighty chose this title for His beloved Son, and you're missing out if you disregard this side of Christ's personality. The Bride cannot really be the Bride without men. Muster up the courage to face your discomfort and misgivings concerning this identity. Oh, how we need your version of passion for Jesus.

With distress increasing rapidly over the face of the earth, we had better find our way into the inner courts of intimacy, now, before the hour of deception has reached a climax. This is the season of preparation when there's opportunity to foster a close personal relationship with our Savior. We must learn to recognize Him as the ultimate Lover instead of just yielding to a vague doctrine of holy matrimony with the Creator. If we are to survive the days ahead and remain steadfast to the Savior, we must develop a strong affection for the Son. We must grow in anticipation of that union.

I have a good friend who has wrestled with this concept. He's married with a beautiful wife and two daughters. Without a doubt, Dan is totally masculine and loves being a man. I still remember when their first daughter was born. I went to the hospital to celebrate her arrival and found a room full of men watching football. Still drowsy from the birth, mom and baby occupied a section of the bed. She found a way to greet me while dad, grandpa, and brothers cheered for the next touchdown. The moment captured the essence of masculinity—adrenalin, competition, and lots of grunting that really means, "This is so much fun."

Dan has talked openly with me about his view of the Bridegroom. It hasn't come easy, but over time he has developed a perspective that works for him. "Jesus, the Bridegroom believes in my potential. He is actively seeking to promote me, placing me in the leadership pipeline. He's my boss who not only hires me, but invites me to dinner." We're not talking about a cheerleader or even a coach. This is a boss with infinite authority and superior influence. Jesus, the Bridegroom pursues you; no other options will He consider. He wants you and *only* you.

Preparing the Way for Christ

In this hour, men of God have the high calling of preparing the way for the Lord's second visit to earth. Inspired by their love for Christ, these are men who take their job seriously as the spiritual leaders of their families. They are true to their wives, treasuring this relationship above any other and partnering with her through daily prayer. They are actively involved in their family's lives, assuming primary responsibility for modeling a devoted passion for Christ to their children. They are men who are careful to develop a reputation of integrity, faithfulness, honesty, and trust. But most of all, they are men who have developed a relationship with their God in their private chambers. He is their source for wisdom, strength, and endurance, as well as their wellspring of security, courage, and optimism.

The world hasn't seen many of these men—yet! Like never before, God is bringing new revelation regarding the infinite love of Christ. It's a depth of love so powerful that its strength can only be compared to the love between a man and woman. It is transparent, personal, and private. This is the love that ignites passion to die for the cause and inspires these men of God to rise up as a superior force before Christ's return.

My husband is a mighty man of God. As an intercessor, I know he's taken the hits for our family on many occasions while regularly praying for our protection. More than once, he has made it known that he would die for us if it ever came to that. He is also a prophet who actively seeks to lead his family in righteousness. He represents us in the public place with integrity. He is a humble man who is mindful of his need for a Savior, but he also has a commanding presence that can bring stability to a room of discord. Most importantly, he has personal communion with God, which gives him the strength and inspiration to lead us. Hank is a model of Christ to many, and my admiration for him grows daily. He is a true friend of the Bridegroom.

Chapter 9

Where the Longing is Finally Satisfied

The Bridegroom's love can best be expressed by the word *longing*. Take a look at an engaged couple. They long to be with one another, to hear from one another, and to share life with one another, continually yearning to end the season of singleness and live together through the bond of a marriage covenant.

That's *exactly* how Christ feels about you! Even though He is with you in spirit, He is still physically separated from you. Your perspective of Christ is limited, at best, because you don't have the advantage of physical interaction enabling your five senses to establish reality: *"Now we see but a poor reflection . . . then we shall see face to face. Now I know in part; then I shall know fully, even as I am fully known"* (1 Corinthians 13:12). He longs to get beyond the formalities of religious etiquette to establish familiarity with you; a "knowing" that only originates from a face-to-face connection. He's waiting to see if you share the same longing for Him.

Jesus Can Relate to the Feeling

Jesus is also single. He knows exactly what it feels like to be lonely. He is very familiar with the intense desire for a mate and the thrust of desperate emotions when the wait feels endless. He is also facing the same challenges of biding time. He is finding ways to stay positive, quietly resisting the intense longing in His heart for someone very special. That someone is you! He longs for you. He wants to be near you, to interact with you, to share life with you. Jesus Christ has you on His mind 24/7, and the only thing that gets Him through the day is the hope that you are also thinking of Him. Remember that part in the Bible when Jesus is performing the first communion? What did He say after He shared the bread and the cup with everyone? *"Remember me."* Man, what a moment that must have been. This is the voice of the Bridegroom, anticipating the physical separation that would exist before His return. Jesus was saying, "Don't forget about me. I won't forget you." When you take a peek into eternal emotions, you will recognize this longing. It is unavoidable.

The only way to sooth a lovesick heart, is to send word. War stories are full of these sentiments. The guy is on the battlefield, fighting to stay alive. The next scene shows his buddy desperately searching for him in the rubble. What's in his hands? A letter from someone who shares his heart. The word from a loved one is the life source. He isn't forgotten; he belongs to someone who cares. Suddenly the will to live is revived. When He remembers you and you remember Him, divine intimacy happens.

The Love of God Is Passionate

The Bride is not gender-specific because the title refers to a spiritual being. The Bride of Christ would not be complete without women *and* men, but the Bible does address the Bride in feminine terminology for one purpose—to help us identify with the quality of Christ's love for His church. Because the Bride is the object of His affection, He desperately longs to be united with her by the Spirit in a relationship that is just as close as the one He has with His Father.

WHERE THE LONGING IS FINALLY SATISFIED

Some people get caught up in the terminology and stop there. I hope you bypass that insidious temptation to see divine intimacy as weird. Although we live in a culture that readily associates passion with lust, there is absolutely nothing perverse about falling in love with the Bridegroom, whether you're a man or woman. Yes, God created sex to be passionate, but sex is not the whole extent of passion. God came up with the idea to help you better understand *His* passion. He has a love for you that is so strong you cannot possibly relate to it without an experience to help you understand at least part of the picture. He knew that the intensity of sexual love would be one of the best ways to describe His passion. He is not a sexual being, but He does have a high intensity of fiery love for you that exceeds anything you've ever experienced on earth. He longs for you to accept and receive that love.

Have you seen Mel Gibson's film *The Passion of the Christ?* When it came out a few years ago, theaters were sold out for days and people waited in long lines for hours before the next showing. Never has there been such a remarkable response from the public with any film.

The movie is a horrific depiction of the last day of Christ's life—two solid hours of brutal torture, betrayal, hatred, and injustice. Honestly, I couldn't watch every scene. The intensity of emotion was too much to bear. How could anyone do that to another human being? Why would God do that for me? The length to which Christ went to prove His love for me was . . . well . . . crazy! I left feeling extreme remorse; *my* sin necessitated His mission. But I was equally dumbfounded. Why am I worth that much to God?

John 17 describes the passion of Christ. It is the only recording of a prayer Jesus prayed in the Garden of Gethsemane just moments before soldiers came to arrest He. This was Christ's last will and testament—the summation of His ultimate purpose and a final plea for what He desired most in life. He asked that the Father might be glorified in His life and prayed for His disciples, but He also prayed for you and me!

"*My prayer is not for them alone. I pray also for those who will believe in me through their message*" (John 17:20). Jesus was praying for the generations of future believers who would eventually accept His love as truth. Can you imagine at that very moment that He had *your* name in mind, and your face actually brought Him comfort? Jesus prayed for *you* that night!

During the time of the greatest testing in His life, Jesus was encouraged to realize that His sacrifice would eventually make a relationship with you possible. Ephesians 1:18 even says that from God's perspective, the voluntary surrender of your life makes Him wealthy with "*the riches of his glorious inheritance in the saints.*" This key phrase specifically identifies the source of His greatest treasure—you! YOU are His prize! According to God, He gained more than you did. Can you feel His pleasure as that truth settles over you? That is the love of the Bridegroom.

Chapter 10
"'Till Death Do Us Part"

During my junior year in college, I began taking private voice lessons. My teacher, Mrs. Norma Heyde, was a beautiful woman whose countenance shone with notable poise and grace. Elegance was her trademark, and she always reminded me of a ballroom dancer. With her angelic demeanor, Mrs. Heyde not only trained the voice, but she also inspired the heart. I was thankful just to sit under her influence.

Eventually I married Hank, graduated, and moved away from the area. Several years later we resettled only to discover we were a few miles from Mrs. Heyde's new home where she and her husband had retired. I resumed weekly lessons, and our relationship began to deepen. She was a woman of faith who loved the Lord with all her heart. Because she didn't have any children of her own, I liked to think that I somehow filled the place of a daughter for her. We used to sit for hours, sharing a cup of tea and talking about life. She always requested that we end the time with prayer.

Love is Stronger than Death

Mrs. Heyde was later diagnosed with lymphoma, and the countenance of her stately figure was gradually overcome by great pain. Wincing turned to screams while she fought to maintain her dignity. Few were permitted to see her in this condition, so we prayed and sent cards. Dr. Heyde cared for his wife throughout her illness. He was there 24/7—repositioning her pillow, fielding phone calls, managing the home, paying the bills—while trying to keep her smiling. No one knew her better. Even though they didn't have any children to help them shoulder this trial, they had each other. Their desperate devotion for one another showed in their eyes—a deep, passionate love that never needed any words. He was her life, and she was his. She lingered on the threshold of death for several months, but the Heydes were still like two sweethearts coming home from a date; the strength and depth of their relationship withstood the interruption of disease.

"Till death do us part." When a devoted couple such as this take their vows to the finish line, married love is never more stunning. Her death was such an undesirable end to their partnership. This was one valley they could not survive together, and Dr. Heyde struggled with the loss for some time. But ultimately, death lost. Their love did not end at the grave because intimacy has an eternal quality. What God has joined together is truly holy.

When Numbers Speak Volumes

It's strange how the sheer numbers of people who make time to attend a funeral tell so much about the kind of life a person has led. No matter how elaborate the program or expensive the reception, people only take time to pay their respects to those who have lived their lives with character. Mrs. Heyde's funeral drew a crowd. The service was magnificent, complete with a string quartet, choir, and organ accompaniment. But most importantly, the service was a testimony to her endearing personality that brought us closer to the love of God. Dr. Heyde had planned the funeral that way. He took a front row seat that day and observed the final tribute to his beloved's life.

Five Categories of People

There are five categories of people at a funeral service. The funeral director prepares the body and helps with the necessary arrangements for the service. His relationship with the deceased is solely from a business perspective. Then there are the friends and business associates of the family members—acquaintances who know the deceased indirectly and have come to show support for the surviving spouse, son, or daughter. Close friends and neighbors comprise yet another group in attendance. These are the ones who had been acquainted with the deceased for years prior to the death. Next are the family members. The common bond of identity and familiarity always draws a family together, regardless of past conflicts, and every member is particularly concerned for the needs of the bereaved. Finally, there is the spouse, the one person in the room who will feel the greatest sense of loss. With billions of people on the planet, absolutely *no one* in the entire world can replace their loved one. They will endure a private grief that is inconsolable. So close is their bond of oneness that the sensation of separation is virtually impossible to comprehend. Their identity will never be the same, especially if their marriage had been defined by intimate companionship.

Jesus Wants a Front Row Seat

Jesus does not want to be the funeral director who you do business with at the end of your life. Neither does He want to be a mere acquaintance that shows concern during your trials of life then moves on with His own life. He wants to mean more to you than a friend or even a close family member. Jesus wants to be the spouse in your life. He wants to be the one in the front row seat. He wants to be the One you turn to at the end of each the day—the one who is your closest companion. That kind of relationship just isn't a given. It's an intimate type of love that happens when the heart of God connects with the heart of man. It's a love that is developed over time, sharing every season of life. Intimacy with Jesus is enjoyed on the mountains of life when things are going great, but it takes on an even deeper meaning when you're struggling through the valleys. Common suffering binds two hearts together, and somehow the fiery trials cause intimacy to thrive and deepen. There is no greater joy than knowing Jesus on this level.

Chapter 11
Focused Passion

I know what you must be thinking right now: *I thought this book was about building relationships.* Teach me about dating boundaries and how to get through this season of singleness. We'll get there, believe me, but I've discovered that young men and women who take notes from the God of romance have a better track record for successful relationships. They have a single-minded focus that will not only secure their bond of faithfulness to a spouse; a bond that prepares them for the difficult times they are certain to experience in their married lives. Young adults of the twenty-first century are going to need a lot more than just relationship skills to overcome the enormous orchestration of satanic strategies to lure them into deception. They will need a life focus that keeps their eyes riveted on the author of love.

Passionate Love Helps You Discern Truth

One day Jesus started talking about the future. He began to describe terrifying events that would eventually take place over the course of history. Jesus was speaking about the times in which we are now living. The Bible text sounds a lot like a CNN script.

"Watch out that no one deceives you. For many will come in my name, claiming, 'I am the Christ' and will deceive many. You will hear of wars and rumors of wars, but see to it that you are not alarmed.

Such things must happen, but the end is still to come. Nation will rise against nation, and kingdom against kingdom. There will be famines and earthquakes in various places. All these are the beginning of birth pains. Then you will be handed over to be persecuted and put to death, and you will be hated by all nations because of me. At that time many will turn away from the faith and will betray and hate each other, and many false prophets will appear and deceive many people. Because of the increase of wickedness, the love of most will grow cold, but he who stands firm to the end will be saved" (Matthew 24:4–13).

Did you catch the degree of deception? **Many** *will turn away!* How do you read this phrase and not feel anxious? *You* may be counted among those who will retreat. Nothing we have experienced thus far in modern America could help us relate to that intense level of testing. The love of family, love for humanity, or even the love for ministry will not be strong enough to contend with the impending temptation to abandon your commitment to Christ. *Intimacy is the only sure inspiration that sustains faith in the midst of trial.*

Another passage gives us even more explicit detail about the days to come.

"They will put you out of the synagogue; in fact, a time is coming when anyone who kills you will think he's offering a service to God. They will do such things because they have not known the Father or me" (John 16:2–3). Jesus is describing a time of such massive deception that religious people will execute Christians, believing that they are doing the will of God. What guarantee do you have that you won't be counted among the deceived? According to this Scripture, it has everything to do with having an intimate relationship with the Father and the Son; a casual relationship will not cut it. He is describing a relationship fostered by personal, one-on-one times in the arms of Jesus.

When your life is threatened, the will to survive commands your actions. Only the devotion of intimacy takes on a superior influence. *"They overcame him by the blood of the Lamb and the word of their testimony; and they did not love their lives so much as to shrink from death"* (Revelation 12:11). This strength of passion will be your single defense against the strategies of Satan to lure you out of God's kingdom.

Wake Up!

We need to wake up! The signs of the times are more than obvious, and we are desperately ignorant of true passion for Christ. Like never before the Lord is calling to anyone who will listen. He is shouting the message, "Get right with Me now, or it will be too late." Jesus will come again. *"For the Lord himself will come down from heaven, with a loud command, with the voice of the archangel and with the trumpet call of God, and the dead in Christ will rise first. After that, we who are still alive and are left will be caught up with them in the clouds to meet the Lord in the air. And so we will be with the Lord forever"* (1 Thessalonians 4:16–17). Jesus is the Bridegroom, and His ravished heart of love is intent on His Bride. The specific hour of His return is a mystery, but the signs are obvious that the time is very near. How do you know if you will be counted among those swept away in His embrace?

When your routine includes attending church and carrying a Bible, somehow there's an assurance that "you're in." After all, you're doing all the right things, right? Not, necessarily. Most of us know far more about Christian culture than we do about God. They are not one and the same. Intimacy is all about relationship that is fostered in private chambers. Knowing God requires time alone with God, without spectators or company. Pressing in to understand a God you cannot see or hear does not sound like fun. No one makes God a priority unless they're desperate—unless they've discovered that nothing, absolutely *nothing* in this world satisfies like God does. Gone are vain pursuits for pleasure, for work, and for more. Jesus is coming for someone who's watching and waiting for Him with desperate anticipation.

When you embrace Jesus as the Bridegroom, you become fixated on the One who loves you. All other earthly dreams and desires no longer distract you. This focus is the place of immunity, where pressures to abandon the faith can't influence you—even in the face of death.

Chapter 12

A Little Parable with a Big Message

"At that time the kingdom of heaven will be like ten virgins who took their lamps and went out to meet the bridegroom."
                                                        Matthew 25:1

Jesus was just like a resident college student. He was away from home and never tired of talking about the place of familiarity. He often referred to it as the "kingdom of heaven." It was not only His way of reminiscing but it was also His worldview. Like you, He considered His earthly existence within the context of where He came from and where He was going. Jesus longed for people to understand His kingdom mindset.

The Time of Preparation

Life on earth is temporary, a space of time between two eternities. Some choose to follow Christ; most do not. But for those who take the higher road of divine purpose, the kingdom of heaven begins on earth. They are waiting for Christ's return—spiritual virgins reserved for divine love. Jesus no longer walks among us, but communion with Christ is made possible through the work of the Holy Spirit. He enables the virgins, young, inexperienced and very vulnerable to learn kingdom mindsets—a vast network of righteous living encased in abundant blessings. But not every virgin recognizes life as the time of preparation.

> *"Five of them were foolish and five were wise. The foolish ones took their lamps but did not take any oil with them. The wise, however, took oil in jars along with their lamps. The bridegroom was a long time in coming, and they all became drowsy and fell asleep."*
>
> Matthew 25:2–5

We take it for granted every time we flip a switch, but before electricity, people had to use oil lamps as a source of light. That meant trimming wicks and purchasing enough oil to keep the lamps burning. It must have been a hassle.

The Challenge of Waiting

When was the last time you had to wait in line? Were you at a tollbooth, a car wash, a bank, or the local Olive Garden? No one likes to wait, especially when you don't have an "expected wait" sign or the traffic is at a dead stop. Without any news from the Bridegroom, it's easy to understand how these virgins got tired of waiting. But half of them spent the time wisely.

> *"At midnight the cry rang out: 'Here's the bridegroom! Come out to meet him!'*
>
> *Then all the virgins woke up and trimmed their lamps. The foolish ones said to the wise, 'Give us some of your oil; our lamps are going out.'*
>
> *'No,' they replied, 'there may not be enough for both us and you. Instead, go to those who sell oil and buy some for yourselves.'*
>
> Matthew 25:6–9

A LITTLE PARABLE WITH A BIG MESSAGE

Divine intimacy produces spiritual oil. It cannot be manufactured, purchased, or borrowed. This is oil that can only be acquired through private time with Jesus. Wise virgins choose to spend time alone with the Lord because they want to, not because they're *supposed* to. The residue of this oil changes your countenance; admiration and respect follows those who make time to foster relationship with Jesus. And it changes your life focus. Desperation for Christ's return grows with increasing intensity. Naturally, the foolish virgins turn to the wise virgins for help, but spiritual oil cannot be donated. The private investment has only one recipient. That's what makes intimacy with Jesus priceless.

Wasting Time

You can't fill a lamp with spiritual oil apart from this priority, but many try. Some virgins pass the time doing little more than religious routine. They go through the motions, unaware that what matters most is relationship. Still others focus on developing interests. They apply their talents to noble exploits in the career fields, fascinated with the challenges of business and even ministry. The steady drumbeat of being busy gradually minimizes the value of spending time with Jesus alone. Service gives the appearance of selfless motives, but in truth these virgins are running from boredom and the pursuit for more fulfillment replaces the pursuit for intimacy. The oil is quickly running out and so is time.

> "But while they were on their way to buy the oil, the bridegroom arrived. The virgins who were ready went in with him to the wedding banquet. And the door was shut. Later the others also came, 'Sir! Sir! they said. Open the door for us!'
> "But he replied, 'I tell you the truth, I don't know you.'"
>
> Matthew 25: 10–12

Knowing God on intimate terms is what it's all about. We are taught what Christ has done for us and what is available to us through His sacrifice; and we are taught what we must do to live within righteous boundaries. But there are few teachings on knowing God. It is a vast subject, but knowing God is what it takes to please God, ultimately.

The only way to know Him is to foster relationship with Him. This is not a natural desire. To pursue a God you cannot see or hear competes with all the other interests in life. But this is the point. Intimacy with Jesus begins with a decision to investigate God's personality. It isn't a well-traveled road. You will not meet many along the path, but this is the ultimate desire of God's heart. He *longs* to be known!

Is your oil lamp full? Time is not on your side. The countdown has already begun. The hour of testing is quickly approaching and only those who have spiritual oil will have reserve power and authority to remain faithful. Tick. Tick. Tick. It's not too late. The question is a matter of your priorities. What will it take for you to make Jesus your first love?

Chapter 13

I Want to Know You the Way You Want to be Known

"I want to know You, Lord, the way You want to be known." I don't remember how old I was when I began to pray this prayer, but it's come across my lips for many years. One day it occurred to me that I could not assume knowing God was even possible. I mean, what if I was imagining a God that did not exist in the context of my perspective? What if I was trying to relate to God the way I thought was right—a mere shot in the dark of sincere intentions? But who was to say if I was even remotely on target? I finally realized that was a waste of time. Simply put, I gave God the job of making Himself known to me. I wanted to know God just the way He wanted to be known. It became a life prayer that settled all the unanswered questions.

You Want to be My Friend?

"You are my friends if you do what I command. I no longer call you servants, because a servant does not know his master's business. Instead I call you friends, for everything that I learned from my Father I have made known to you."

John 15:14-15

To know Him the way He wanted to be known was far different from the relationship I had pictured. Saying "Yes" to divine love takes you past a mere servant role. Selfless consideration of others should never change, but Jesus is qualifying a much closer relationship with you, personally. He wants to confide in you, becoming much more friendly than a master/servant arrangement. That request changed everything for me—my religion would never be the same. I had to know this God who wanted to be close to me, who actually enjoyed me. But one question remained: Did I enjoy *Him?* I didn't know how to answer that question honestly, but I kept praying this prayer with great sincerity.

It wasn't long before I began to experience an increased desire for Him . . . strange how we cannot muster that desire on our own. It didn't come as a tidal wave, really. It was more like a sprinkle—a steady stream of mist that was intentionally temporary. I had the satisfaction of God's presence in my life, but I could never hold on to it for long. It wasn't an investment that I could deposit in a bank and withdraw from when I needed it. No, this was an experience that lasted one day at a time.

As long as I prayed this prayer with a sincere heart, I had the assurance of His company. His companionship was so satisfying that I longed for more. He never left me, but I could feel Him closer when I took time to foster my relationship with Him. Eventually daily prayer and reading my Bible became a consistent part of my daily routine. My desire was growing.

The Bridegroom Longs To Be Pursued

The daily provision runs out because Jesus longs to be pursued. What lover doesn't? Isn't that the key ingredient in every love story? Liturgy in a prayer book won't satisfy His desire for intimacy with you. No, He wants so much more than religious routine. He wants you to develop a curiosity about His personality. He is waiting for you to ask for the clues to a treasure hunt of divine desire.

One day I asked God to help me get to know Him better. I was a little frustrated, almost bored with what I already knew about God. I desperately wanted to know Him more, but I couldn't figure out how to get past the ordinary. All at once, various intriguing thoughts flashed through my mind as I reflected on His earthly personality.

Jesus was human and must have had mannerisms that easily identified Him as Joseph's son. Was He right- or left-handed? When He walked down the street, how did His friends recognize Him from behind? What were His favorite foods? How did He handle a sniffle? Did He whistle when He was content? What did His laugh sound like, and what were the inside jokes He shared with His disciples? There were a hundred questions that I couldn't answer without seeing Him face-to-face. I didn't want to rely on imagination anymore. I really wanted to *experience* Him.

The Pea-Sized Experience

God finally responded to me with a humorous statement: "All that you know about Me could fit into a pea!" I shook my head and raised my eyebrows. Deep down in my heart, I knew I had heard Him correctly. The statement was so odd that I couldn't possibly have thought the words for God; I didn't even say, "What?" For a moment I paused, and then I began to focus on the size of a pea.

If all of my experiential knowledge of God could fit into a pea, then there must be so much more to discover, I mused. Almost instantly, I imagined that my hand was full of peas, each representing forty years of a totally new experience with God. Then I visualized a bucket of them spilling over, covering the floor. I watched, rather speechless as the peas began to fill the entire room!

Enthralled by the amazing vision, my thoughts abruptly turned to the science unit of a book about the planets that we used to homeschool our children. One page explained how a satellite had been sent to study Pluto, the planet furthest from the sun. When the satellite finally reached its destination, it would have traveled nine years! I was impressed by that fact, marveling at the vast expanse of our solar system, which is relatively small compared to other galaxies in the universe.

While I was meditating on Pluto, suddenly the peas of my previous vision stretched out into a large cord toward the direction of the sky. I realized that the line of peas was headed to Pluto, and the revelation of God's infinite love flooded my soul. It was an indescribable feeling. God's love is limitless, and eternity will never be long enough to fully experience Him. I was filled with so much joy that I screamed out, "Give me a cantaloupe, Lord!" I didn't want just a pea—I wanted a cantaloupe-sized experience with Him. (This explains the odd request I sometimes make of God during corporate worship. "I want a cantaloupe!" does not exactly fit the meditative mood in church when we're singing, "This is the air I breathe." But it happens to be an inside joke between God and me.) How He longs to be known by you—to take you beyond a pea-sized experience.

Chapter 14

Who is God, Anyway?

Who is God? This question brings us closer to a true experience with God. We've been taught so much about what God has done for us and what we can receive from His provision. We also know a great deal about what we are expected to do as His followers, but few of us study who God really is.

Most of us don't view God as a being with a personality, but He is very intriguing. Let me challenge you to investigate *who God is*. The adventure will change your life.

God is Jealous

Jealousy is one particular facet of His personality that has a direct bearing on the way to build healthy relationships. When you begin to understand this characteristic of God you'll fully appreciate the need for His involvement in your relationships, especially for your future marriage. No one enjoys the journey of romance when a threat of competition exists. Thus, love must establish the trust needed to keep jealousy at bay, or it won't succeed. As the Bridegroom, Jesus has a possessive nature: *"For the LORD your God is a consuming fire, a jealous God"* (Deuteronomy 4:24). He is unwilling to share you with any other pursuit.

Since we were made in the image of God, it's comforting to know that when we experience jealousy, He fully understands the emotion. Of course, I am validating godly jealousy as a righteous character trait. There is a fleshly form of jealousy based on irrational fear that often stems from previous wounds of rejection. Jealousy of this kind leads to sinful methods of manipulation and control as a false antidote; godly jealousy, on the other hand, is a righteous expectation of *exclusive love*. God thought it was right to share this emotion with man.

God Is Very Jealous for You

"This is what the LORD Almighty says: 'I am very jealous for Zion; I am burning with jealousy for her'" (Zechariah 8:2). In this text, the Lord communicates His jealousy to the people of Israel because they turned from Him to seek after foreign gods, just as they had done many times in the past. Idolatry has the same effect on God that adultery has on a marriage. When you choose another "god" to worship and follow, it hurts the Lord, just as if you cheated on your spouse. Anything that replaces God or competes with Him in your life is considered an idol. One of the best ways to measure your heart's affections is to look at how you spend your time and money. Your daily planner and your checkbook give an accurate account of what your heart truly treasures.

When Paul addressed the church in Corinth, he was deeply concerned that they continued to dabble in idolatry and compared it to the grief experienced by a spouse whose partner committed adultery. He states, *"I am jealous for you with a godly jealousy. I promised you to one husband, to Christ, so that I might present you as a pure virgin to him"* (2 Corinthians 11:2). **Godly jealousy is a God-inspired component of love designed to protect the holiness of matrimony.** It's like a built-in alarm that is activated whenever trust is compromised and involves a feeling that cannot be resisted, only prevented.

The strength of godly jealousy comes with knowing God intimately. When you realize the jealous love God has for you, your focus becomes the pursuit of eliminating anything and anyone that would compete with His place in your life. This effort secures your inheritance.

How Does God Fit Into a Relationship?

When Hank and I were first married, we had such a strong love for one another, and we were both serious about working on our faith. There was no question that God was a big part of our lives and that we wanted His direction for our marriage. We just didn't understand *how* God would fit into our marriage.

Hank was raised listening to oldies from the '60s. In fact, this kind of music greatly influenced his beliefs about love. He really believed the words in those love songs represented truth. Most of them portrayed the false assurance that human love could withstand any test. He put a lot of faith in my love for him—much more than I could guarantee. Subconsciously, he viewed me as his source for love. Yes, he knew Jesus as his Savior and Lord, but he saw me as God's provision for that love, which made for a very unbalanced emotional scale in our relationship.

Most people marry with the misconception that love will find its fulfillment in one another, but men and women were not created to be each other's source of love. Our need for love is far too deep for that. In fact, only God is capable of filling our love tanks. God designed us for His love alone, and He is the only One who can completely satisfy our needs. When our focus is centered on His jealous love for us, love for our spouse flows in abundance.

The triangle in the diagram below is a great illustration of this spiritual principle. If God is at the apex and a husband and wife are at the two base corners, you can see that God fits perfectly as the love source for either partner. As both partners individually pursue God in their personal relationships with Him, they will begin to grow closer to Him. The closer they are to God, the closer they become as a couple.

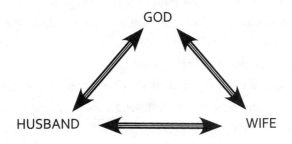

Chapter 15

So How Do You Relate to an Invisible God?

We've been talking a lot about the love of God, but what does it take to actually develop a close relationship with the Almighty? It's really not as hard as it might appear. Moses had to climb a mountain, fast from food and water for forty days, endure the billowing smoke he compared to a furnace, and maintain his balance while the mountain quaked—possibly standing a few feet above a volcano that was about to burp. That's all. Thankfully, Jesus made a way for us to communicate with Him without as many obstacles. You just might find it to be fun!

God Wants To Be Noticed

Most of all, God desires your attention. He loves it when you start noticing Him in everyday life and including Him in your activities. *"Because he loves me," says the LORD, "I will rescue him; I will protect him, **for he acknowledges my name**"* (Psalm 91:14).

He simply wants to be recognized—to be acknowledged throughout the day. He deserves the credit for *everything* that is good in your life. He loves to hear you say, "That's God for 'ya. Isn't He awesome?" When you have a growing relationship with God, you're going to talk about Him and look for ways to point Him out. He loves that.

God Wants to Spend Time with You

When you love someone, you also want to spend time with them. The same is true of your relationship with God. I highly recommend that you make it a priority to regularly meet with God at a specific time of day. Life in America is busy and hurried, but there isn't a fast-food line to intimacy with God. Building a relationship with God doesn't work when you squeeze Him into your schedule. Take a good look at your schedule and determine a set time of day that will work for you. Start with fifteen minutes a day. You can always add more minutes later, but this time frame is "doable," at least when you're first getting started. Make sure you find a place that is quiet and private. Sometimes that can be a challenge. When my children were young, I had to wake up very early in the morning to get a living room seat all to myself. Often times I had to resort to the bathroom—God will even meet you there. Just look for a quiet time and place to meet alone with God to share your thoughts.

During those fifteen minutes, spend time in prayer and reading the Bible. Prayer is simply talking to God. To help me stay focused, I always pray out loud. It really helps me articulate my emotions, the place where the longings of my heart are lodged. I always try to put a title to the feeling. This is very therapeutic, and it commonly gives you access to communicate with a spiritual God. I usually begin by telling God what I'm feeling at the time. "For some reason I feel depressed today, God," or "God, I'm really feeling overwhelmed today," or "I love being loved by you, God!" There are thousands of emotions, and God loves to hear you describe them. I try to identify what I'm really feeling and talk to God about it.

The key to a close walk with God is being *real* with Him. Don't use published prayers unless they're written in first person. He wants to hear exactly what you talk to a friend about. You know, the one you spend an hour on the phone talking about, well—stuff. That's exactly what interests God! He wants to hear about every detail in your life, even the crazy nonessentials. I don't spend this time praying for the needs of others. I do pray for people as the Lord puts them on my heart, but this is really time reserved for just God and me. Generally, we talk about my life, and then I listen to what's on His mind.

God Wants to Speak to You

Reading the Bible is the other key to spending time alone with God because He wants to respond to you. I may not hear Him at that very moment, but I try to meditate on the Scripture I read throughout the whole day. On some days the passage is more relevant than others, but I'm amazed at how God uses every text I read, even if He chooses to expound on it several months down the road. If you find the Bible boring or confusing, ask God to help you develop a fascination with Scripture. You might start by reading the Gospels (Matthew, Mark, Luke, John) or maybe the Psalms; all five of these books are interesting and full of encouragement.

By the way, the Bible is a book of many books that are written by different authors. And each author has a different style with a different target audience. Some are poets, some are historians, and some are prophets, but each author's writings are grouped together. Consequently, the Bible is not organized in chronological order. You can begin reading at the beginning, but the books do not follow a consistent story line like most books do.

Another thing too . . . there are many different versions of the Bible. There is only *one* Holy Bible, but the original manuscripts were written in Hebrew and Greek. Accurate translation is a meticulous process because language similarities are not exact. Additionally, much of the Bible was written in the context of the Middle Eastern civilization. Therefore, translation of the original documents into the English language and culture is a collective effort on the part of many notorious scholars. Any Christian bookstore will carry the latest, up-to-date versions and they are all excellent resources, each communicating a consistent message. It's also a good idea to take advantage of Bible studies or classes. This is a great way to learn how to understand what the Bible is saying to you. Campus ministries typically host such meetings. These would be well worth your time, especially if you've never read the Bible.

The Bible is complete truth. There isn't anything better that can get you heading in the right direction. The Bible is a treasure chest waiting to be discovered, and the search to understand His Word will cause your relationship with Him to grow. Ask God questions and expect answers. God will *always* speak in absolute agreement with His word. This is the best way to know if the voice you're hearing is really God.

Chapter 16

God Wants to Talk with You

We were created in the image of God. Stop. Now, just think about that. When you look in the mirror, you actually see an image of what God looks like. He doesn't have your complexion—the color and texture of His skin is probably a little more radiant—but the shape of a human being is similar to the shape of God. He has hands and feet, a neck and a head and waist. The book of Revelation describes some very interesting creatures in heaven, but we look a lot like the important One on the throne! That means that God has five senses. He has the capacity to see, hear, touch, smell, and taste. Consequently, He does not simply rely upon the spoken word when He has something to say. He has far more variety than that, often using scenery, sound, textures, aromas, and flavors to communicate His love to us.

Vision—Acts 2:3 says, *"They saw what seemed to be tongues of fire that separated and came to rest on each of them."* This must have been the most thrilling experience. The apostles and many of the devoted had gathered together in a room for a prayer meeting. Suddenly, a violent wind swept through the house. I can just imagine that it looked a lot like Dorothy in her bedroom when the tornado hit. Most likely, doors slammed, chairs crashed to the floor, and dust swirled around their tousled hair. Before they could even speak, flames of fire the size of torches came from nowhere, separated all by themselves, and hovered over each one of them. What a scene that must have been! God was demonstrating His power, and He had something important to say. Even though we are not told that an audible voice was heard, the flames of fire represented the Holy Spirit. He ignited in each of them and then manifested Himself through their mouths, uttering foreign languages that others could understand.

God still speaks through visions as well as the ordinary events of daily life. Many times over, I have asked God for guidance, and He places a visual answer directly in front of me. One day, I remember spending a prolonged time in prayer. I was confused and felt falsely accused, but I could not discern what truth was. In desperation, I asked Him to make it clear whether I was contending with evil or in need of repentance. Within moments of finishing the prayer, I walked out to my dining room window and saw a red fox running right across my yard. Foxes are nocturnal animals, so they usually aren't seen in the early afternoon. I knew instinctively that God had confirmed the presence of evil and was warning me to proceed with caution. Peace flooded my heart as I realized that God was talking to me. *God loves to speak, and He loves to be heard.*

Hearing—"*One day at about three in the afternoon he had a vision. He distinctly saw an angel of God, who came to him and said, 'Cornelius!'*" (Acts 10:3). In many biblical stories, God speaks with a voice that can be heard, but this is one time when a man is specifically addressed by name. Have you ever heard God speak your name? I've never heard an audible voice, but He does speak my name so I can hear it in my heart. I live to hear His voice because there is nothing else like it this side of heaven.

Revelation 1:15 tells us that His voice is like *"the sound of rushing waters."* Can you imagine hearing, "I love you!" coming from the waters of Niagara Falls? Millions of gallons of water spilling over the steep rock ledges, making such a thunderous sound that you couldn't carry on a conversation—now *that* would be a pretty convincing love message. Even though He probably toned it down for Cornelius, God has a voice. And He uses it to communicate with us. God regularly comments on the events of your life. Whether it's a still whisper in your heart or an audible voice from the choir loft, *God loves to speak, and He loves to be heard.*

Touch—*"When Elizabeth heard Mary's greeting, the baby leaped in her womb, and Elizabeth was filled with the Holy Spirit"* (Luke 1:41). This was Elizabeth's first and last pregnancy. Even though she was a senior citizen, God had miraculously opened her womb. Elizabeth was carrying the greatest prophet of the day, John the Baptist, who would foretell the coming of the Messiah. And he started "speaking" at a very young age! Even before he was born, John heard the voice of Mary and leapt in his mother's womb in anticipation of Christ's birth. God was speaking through touch to communicate this message of confirmation and praise to Elizabeth.

The angel told Joseph in a dream that Mary would conceive and bear a son; he was to call Him Immanuel (Matthew 1:23). The name means "God with us." I've always loved Christmas, and my family and friends know that I usually start a countdown in June. As I've grown in my relationship with the Lord, however, it dawned on me that the celebration of God's presence coming to earth is the true source of my joy.

Immanuel is the composite of God's presence, and I have a distinct sensation whenever He is near. Regardless of the season, His presence reminds me of snuggling under a big, downy quilt with a cup of hot tea in front of a fireplace. The best way to describe it is "cinnamony joy," and it makes me feel comforted and much loved. Rarely does He say anything to me, but He doesn't have to. His love is transmitted through this sensation, and it is wonderful. *God loves to speak, and He loves to be heard.*

Smell—My kids especially love it when I hang sheets out on the clothesline to dry. Miraculously, a refreshing fragrance collects between the linens; we call it the smell of heaven. Downy has never been able to duplicate the scent to perfection. Whether it's pumpkin pie baking in the oven, the pine from freshly cut evergreens, or the earthy smell after a spring rain, we love pleasant aromas. There is something powerful about them.

"*And when he had taken it, the four living creatures and the twenty-four elders fell down before the Lamb. Each one had a harp and they were holding golden bowls full on incense, which are the prayers of the saints*" (Revelation 5:8). Did you know that your prayers are communicated to God through smell? He could have used an intercom system to hear our prayers or even a video contraption that would televise our faces when we pray. He could have created a huge room with angels serving as computer operators to dispatch requests. Why would God choose the aroma of incense to communicate our prayers? Because a fragrance *lingers,* and God loves to be constantly reminded of you.

Remember Mrs. Heyde, my voice teacher? I still have several scarves of hers, even though she died in the early 90's. When I unzip the plastic bag where I keep them, I can still smell her perfume, and it comforts me. Collecting your prayers in a golden bowl of incense portrays the true nature of a romantic Lover who misses His Bride. "*But thanks be to God, who always leads us in triumphal procession in Christ* *and through us spreads everywhere the **fragrance** of the knowledge of him"* (2 Corinthians 2:14). Jesus is the ultimate Lover and when you communicate with Him, His fragrance rubs off on your countenance. God loves to speak, and He loves to be heard.

Taste —There is no better time to relate to God through taste than when you celebrate the sacrament of communion. In ancient times, Middle Eastern cultures had a custom called the Wine Banquet to recognize a formal marriage proposal. During the ceremony, the man would pour wine into a cup, symbolizing an agreement to selflessly love his betrothed—even unto death if it was ever asked of him. In response, the woman would drink of the cup to signify her acceptance of the proposal to love, honor, and remain faithful to their marriage covenant.

Typically, we do not view the Last Supper as a Wine Banquet, but that is exactly what Jesus had in mind the night before His death. Jesus said, *"I have eagerly desired to eat this Passover with you before I suffer. For I tell you, I will not eat it again until it finds fulfillment in the kingdom of God"* (Luke 22:15–16). **Nowhere** else in Scripture does Jesus specifically say, "I have eagerly desired" *anything!* But this was a highly significant occasion, and He had a confirmation to make—a secured engagement with His Bride. As Jesus poured wine into the cup and said, *"This cup is the new covenant in my blood, which is poured out for you"* (Luke 22:20), He was referring to the covenantal relationship of marriage with the church and prophesying His intentions to one day return for her.

Every time we celebrate Holy Communion *we proclaim His death until He comes again* (1 Corinthians 11:26), the bridal response to His proposal. That's why Paul specifically designates this sacrament only for Christians who surrender their lives to Christ (1 Corinthians 11:29).

This ceremony is all about Jesus and the Bride, and no one else is welcome to participate without incurring judgment upon themselves. As we eat the bread and drink the cup, we "remember Him," thus communicating our choice to wait for His return in faithful submission. *"Taste and see that the LORD is good"* (Psalm 34:8). *God loves to speak, and He loves to be heard.*

Acknowledge His variety and observe every detail with all your senses. You don't want to miss His voice.

Chapter 17

Winning the Battle of Unbelief

Do you remember the movie *Hook?* You know Robin Williams plays Peter Pan and Dustin Hoffman plays Hook. It's an adaptation of the fairy tale set in modern times. Robin Williams is an adult Peter Pan who has completely disengaged from his former identity. He can't remember anything about fighting pirates with a band of misfit boys.

Captain Hook, the villain of Never Never Land is bored. In Peter's absence, the thrill of combat has made him restless so he kidnaps Peter's kids, hoping to instigate a battle. But when Peter arrives, he is far from the threat Hook once knew. This arch rival is now a wimp with deflated adrenalin. "Where's my war?" Hoffman yells with a sourpuss expression. Tinkerbell eventually convinces him to give them three days to prepare Peter for battle. Meanwhile Hook strategizes to find an evil jab—something "below the belt" that would abolish the satisfaction of victory for Pan. Jack, Peter's son becomes the target. If Hook can persuade Jack to doubt his dad's love, defeat of the heart will be sure.

The Influence of Unbelief

From where we stand, Jesus knows His love seems "too good to be true." It's a struggle for human beings to relate to the unconditional terms because we are pitifully vulnerable to the flesh and constantly weakened by sin's influence. Yes, there is exceptional love available for each one of us but so often we fail to enjoy it because we can't justify the gift.

When someone gives you a present it usually comes with a reason. It is customary to exchange birthday and Christmas gifts, but few enjoy an unexpected gift without feeling the urge to return the favor. God's love is lavish—just about the volume of Niagara Falls. We are undeserving of such generosity. There's *no* way to justify it and there's *no* way to give back anything close to comparable. But God longs for us to simply believe it and receive it. **Intimate love is never satisfied until it is received**. That's where Satan comes in.

It's Not About You

When you consider the magnificence of the galaxy, men and women hardly compete with the glories of creation. Yes, we happen to be human beings living and thriving on the only planet that can sustain life, but we are so insignificant in contrast to the limitless expanse of the entire universe. We are frail, fickle, and very fatiguing. Why would Satan spend so much energy interfering in our lives? Why would this enemy remain focused on generations of people who are so easy to control? He doesn't even gain the thrill of a good fight when he plans to destroy our health, wealth, and destiny. Why would Satan waste his time on such weakness? His prize is *not* wounded people in the face of defeat. What he wants is a wounded Savior in the face of our doubt. He's the Hook of mankind.

You're Just What He Wants

We just happen to be the object of God's affection. Satan doesn't have that figured out and neither do we, but the truth of the matter is that we are everything God wants. God could have chosen to set His heart on turtles, toucans, or even rocks on the surface of Neptune. Had He made the flamingo the object of his affection, I can promise you that we would have had absolutely no problem with an enemy—unless, of course, we got between Satan and those pink birds with long legs.

God loves human beings, and He's especially partial to men and women who have surrendered their lives to Him. Voluntary relationship is His ultimate delight. There isn't *anything* that pleases God more. Regardless of failures, a devoted heart makes God smile.

The Hook

God's pleasure is precisely Satan's target. He wants to minimize God's joy. He devises endless schemes by exploiting our weaknesses. First he leads us into sinful distractions with enticing promises. Disobedience is followed by an instant response: the trap door slams shut, and you are completely enslaved to incessant voices of hopelessness.

"You only know how to hurt people."

"You'll never live it down."

"You can't be trusted."

"You're useless."

"You were never wanted."

"You can't change."

When someone deals with sin, a normal progression happens. Guilt leads to condemnation. Condemnation leads to a sense of unworthiness. Finally, unworthiness leads to withdrawal. Anywhere along this path, Jesus stands ready to pull you out of the deception that says His love won't stand, but the hand of faith is hard to grasp when you're struggling with doubt. By emphasizing our failures, Satan "hooks us" with doubt and effortlessly points in the direction of abandoned faith. The devil savors victory with a guttural smile as God begins to cry.

Don't Let Hook Win!

I visualize Jesus running alongside you in the marathon of life. He knows that you've failed and sees your discouragement. He's shouting, "I still love you. I know you didn't mean it. I forgive you. Leave the mistake and take up the lesson. I'm still proud of you. I still love you!" But most of the time, you don't hear Him. Even when you do, you disregard His voice as simple imagination and kick yourself for ever having the audacity to believe it was true in the first place.

Sin *cannot* alter your position with Christ. The Bible clearly states this concept as fact, but it is very hard to believe when your flesh wins. God's love is not logical; it makes far more sense to discard a weak, sin-prone life than to desire Him. But the truth is, God *loves* people. Even in our weakness, Christ loves us enough to say, "You're just what I want, please don't leave me." Don't let Hook win. Just believe.

Part 2

Human Intimacy

Jesus replied,
"'Love the Lord your God with all your heart
and with all your soul and with all your mind.'
This is the first and greatest commandment.
And the second is like it: 'Love your neighbor as yourself.'"

MATTHEW 22:37–39

You're standing on the edge of a high cliff overlooking a canyon—the Canyon of Failed Love. Thousands upon thousands of people are stuck here; people who tried romance and never made it to the place of intimate love. Your life journey has led you to this cliff—every twenty-something's path does. Turning back is not an option. You must move forward, but the probability of relationship failure is overwhelming. Isn't there any way around this canyon? Yes! Oh, yes there most certainly is. God the Creator designed men and women for intimacy. It can happen, but most of the world doesn't understand how it works.

In one statement Jesus summed up the wisdom of all prophets, teachers, and lawyers concerning relationships, in two commandments: #1 *Love the Lord your God with all your heart, soul, mind and strength;* and #2, *Love your neighbor as yourself.* You were designed to have love needs that only God can meet. God intended for you to have a close relationship with Him—one that is intimate and private. This relationship is what stabilizes you, providing enough security so human relationship is not as risky. In the first part of this book, I addressed the process of developing an intimate relationship with Jesus Christ, the ultimate Lover of your soul.

And now we come to the second commandment—human intimacy. It is an exciting journey of discovery that begins in the Garden of Eden.

Chapter 18

The Way We Were

Barbra Streisand sang the song, but God designed the original plan for the way we were supposed to enjoy love. What you know about love is really a tossed salad of observations. Whether you grew up in a home with two loving parents who are still married or an absent father who never cared, your view of love was primarily shaped by what your parents modeled for you. Also, thousands of subliminal messages circulating through today's media and entertainment industries dictate the norms for our culture, particularly in the area of romance. Subconsciously, you sort through all these observations to develop a framework of beliefs about love that register as fact.

Your beliefs have a powerful influence over your view of relationships. What you believe about the opposite sex and expect from a relationship becomes your guide for what's acceptable and what isn't. God cares deeply about your relationships; He knows that you are entering the crucial years for making the most important decisions of your life. Choosing a career path and a mate to share that journey are serious decisions that can be terrifying.

God longs to show you the way of abundant joy and peace that comes through the divine counsel of His Word. He's given you a guide that is much more dependable than your own standards for true love. The Bible has superior wisdom on the topic of relationships, and, contrary to popular opinion, the Book offers a far more fascinating description of human love. Complete with specific directions for finding the ultimate love experience, God's Word even guarantees substantial fulfillment when its principles are followed. To grasp this truth, we need to go back to the way we were. We need to take a look at the blueprint—what God had in mind when a man and woman fall in love.

"The Way We Were" design involved a clear understanding of God's desire to relate to man personally.

Everything about the seven-day Creation story indicates that God truly enjoyed Himself, especially the companionship He shared with Adam. This was not a God who chose to be distant, formal, or sterile. He didn't spend all of His time looking through a magnifying glass at His little man-child as if he were a specimen walking around a terrarium. God actually went down to join him!

Genesis 3:8 tells us that Adam could hear God walking through the garden in the early morning. Maybe God was a mist or perhaps a bright light or a shadow, but somehow He responded to gravity just like we do. He walked around the garden enough that Adam recognized Him passing by. Adam also talked with God regularly, so their relationship was very close. In fact, Genesis 3:9 almost sounds like God is playing hide-and-seek.

God did not create man, place him in the garden, and say, "There, now you figure out the rest." No, God created man to coexist with Him in a relationship that we call divine intimacy.

Yet man wanted another human being to relate to—a human partner whom he could see and touch. Every male animal had a female counterpart, so it was not hard to observe the imbalance. However, no other animal in creation shared God's image. In all the animal kingdom, there was absolutely no other suitable partner for Adam, so God found a way to give man what he longed for without depleting his unique identity as God's offspring.

When God created Adam, He created him in His likeness with a composite of male and female attributes. To meet Adam's need, God extracted the female side of His likeness and placed it in a human body called woman. God formed Eve differently from any other creature. She was not a new creation— she was an extension of the original design. She had a different shape but a similar form that was a perfect counterpart to man. They were created to complement one another, each having corresponding strengths and weaknesses that enhanced their attraction and desire for one another. Together, they possessed an undeniable resemblance to the God who created them.

The strength of Adam and Eve's love for each other was dependent upon their personal, devotional relationship to God. For them, "normal" meant communing with God on an individual level because they regarded Him as the primary source of their love. They regularly enjoyed an overflow of that love and were accustomed to living life with unconditional acceptance from God. It must have been a phenomenal existence!

"The Way We Were" design included an appreciation for their distinct gender differences.

Because Adam and Eve were a composite of God's character, one could not exist apart from the other without failing to portray the fullness of God's expressed love. This does not mean that single men and women cannot access the love of God, but the love between a husband and wife was to be an exhibition of God's completion. Gender differences were intentional, creating a vacuum of appreciation for the opposite sex. Life was to be lived as a team, relying on one another for their God-given strengths.

Men are blessed with strong physical features. Their upper body has muscle mass designed for endurance. Men have thicker skin, enhancing their pain threshold, and they also have thicker skulls. The male anatomy is consistent with their aggressive tendency that lends itself to contact sports, problem solving, and reckless behavior (better known as "fun"!) Men are "left brain thinkers"; they approach challenges logically with clear "cause and effect" solutions. Self-esteem is defined by a man's ability to succeed at a task; achievement reinforces their sense of worth, power, and competence. Lastly, men process life through what is tangible. They talk about concrete events such as projects, sports, news, sex, and work.

In comparison, women were designed with soft features. Their skin tones and hair distribution is designed to emulate the beauty of God. Her greatest strength lies in a maternal instinct. Women can bear children and love them through every growth stage with great determination. There are four times as many brain cells in a female, giving them an ability to access right brain intellect. As a result, women are highly relational, always looking to build friendships and resolve conflicts. Women also process life emotionally. Feelings are a huge grid that determines outlook, perspective, and attitude.

"The Way We Were" design placed a high priority on God's involvement in the marriage relationship as the ultimate source of love.

God knew that Adam and Eve would never reach the fullness of love without His help. *We* (learned how to) *love, because He first* (modeled) *loved* (for) *us* (1 John 4:19). Again, the triangle is a perfect example of the balanced life God intended for men and women from the beginning. God is placed at the highest pinnacle, maintaining superiority in purpose, control, and influence; the husband and wife are set at either corner below God. As Adam and Eve ascended to greater levels of intimacy with God, they inevitably grew closer to each other in human love. Neither man nor woman was ever designed to function independently from God. It was a magnificent plan, and God called it "very good."

God was the absolute object of Adam and Eve's affections, but now they had a physical way to express a spiritual reality. Their physical features were designed for perfect union—one penetrated and the other absorbed in such a way that their original oneness could be reenacted. Within this union, God incorporated His greatest likeness as a life-giver. *"Be fruitful and increase in number; fill the earth and subdue it"* (Genesis 1:28) were the instructions for God's blessing. Endless genetic combinations ensured that human reproduction would always produce an unlimited variety of the species. No two would ever be alike. God determined this prototype for a healthy family—one man and one woman, modeling gender differences within the security of a marriage covenant. Parents would train their children in the ways of God, equipping them for leadership, and the cycle would begin again.

God's Plan for Humanity Included His Son

Nevertheless, God had a much bigger picture in mind than just two humans falling in love with one another; He longed for the consolidation of affection from millions of human beings. The vast numbers of people from every race and generation serving God and loving God would eventually accumulate into a power source of extraordinary love—a passionate love that would satisfy the longing in His Son for a soul mate. God calls this accumulation of love "The Bride of Christ." The fullness of its meaning is profoundly beyond reach. Nevertheless, the Word of God opens and closes with wedding scenes that grandly display the unmistakable romantic nature of God's heart.

Chapter 19

The Way We Are

As the story goes, *"the way we were"* is not the way we stayed. I think God planned it that way...

Love in its simplest form is voluntary. You cannot convince someone to love you through bargaining, guilt, or persuasion—that's control. To be called love, it must be offered willingly. That's why God created man with a free will. He wanted to relate to man very closely, but in order for the essence of that relationship to be defined by love, He had to give man the right to choose.

A Regrettable Decision

There were two trees standing in the middle of the garden—The Tree of Life and the Tree of the Knowledge of Good and Evil (Genesis 2:9). The latter tree presented Adam with the choice to either obey or disobey God. He could eat fruit from any of the other thousands of trees in Paradise, but God specifically told him not to eat from the Tree of Knowledge of Good and Evil.

In the face of temptation, Adam and Eve chose sin; they took a bite of the forbidden fruit. Disobedience always comes with repercussions, and in this case it meant a huge loss. Their sin caused spiritual separation from God. God's love remained constant, but their perception of His love would never be as sure. They would now have to exercise faith above and beyond the crippling messages of doubt, fear, and shame in order to believe that His love was real.

I think God must have known they would not pass the test. He must have predicted their response because He had a backup plan. Mercifully, God chose to banish them from the Garden to prevent them from eating of the Tree of Life (Genesis 3:22–24). That tree had been created to sustain them eternally in a world filled with goodness. He did not want to leave mankind in an unredeemable position of sin, so He permanently exiled them from the Garden. From then on, life would involve a journey of choices surrounded by the influence of evil and the power of temptation. Access to God would only come through a sacrificial system designed to atone for sin so that man's relationship with Him might be restored. But God also had a plan to ultimately win the heart of men.

Passion

Paradise would have been really nice, but apart from sin, how could we have ever known the fullness of love? To experience forgiveness, you've got to have a reason to say I'm sorry. God knew that man would disobey, given the choice, but sin brought the necessary ingredients for passion. Without a need for the Savior, there can be no identification with unconditional love. Yes, it was God's idea to send His Son, but most importantly, it was Christ's desire to redeem His Bride. Paradise would have allowed for an arranged marriage with the courteous formalities of a superficial relationship, but Jesus wanted so much more than that. His love is fiery and passionate with a longing for exchange. The only way to get her attention, ignite her desire, and gain her devotion was to allow her to fail; then He would sacrifice His life to win her back. In the face of unmerited love, passion will thrive.

A Cursed Existence

It would take a long time before Christ arrived on the scene, but there's still so much to learn from Adam and Eve's story. When they chose to disobey God's command it radically changed their worldview. Satan now had permission to influence their minds with destructive thoughts of doubt and shame by using every form of evil. Their weak faith had never been tested before. Satan definitely had the advantage, but this provided them with a personal experience with sin's influence. There's no better way to develop hate for sin than to face regret.

With Adam and Eve's sin came the condition of a cursed existence. Even though they themselves were not cursed, the world in which they lived would be forever tainted. Life would now include sickness, pain, and death. Under the curse's influence, gender differences became pronounced, giving way to division and strife. Relationships were now defined by the process of sorting through a myriad of feelings and opinions, each reflecting a radically different worldview. Agreement would not come naturally as it did before.

Evidence of the curse is still at work today. Regardless of your age, gender, or race people still struggle to resolve their own guilt, and it interferes with choices that impact relationships. Although Christ came to earth to pay the price for our sin, the curse's influence continues to be a stumbling block for even the most faithful servant. The curse has made differences between men and women far more pronounced, giving place to frustration and discord. Relationship is not easy. But even in the midst of these challenges, God comes to help us learn from our mistakes.

Hope is realized in the light of truth. What was the curse's immediate effect on men and women? The answer to this question is found in Genesis. Graciously, God warned Adam and Eve about what they would face—the fundamental explanation for all human conflict.

Chapter 20

How the Curse Affected Women

God created men and women with several innate needs that only He could fulfill—namely purpose and acceptance. While in the Garden of Eden, God took care of making sure those needs were met. Adam and Eve were most likely oblivious to the psychology of those needs, having never experienced anything to the contrary.

However, when they chose to sin, life was forever altered by a cursed existence. Man's need for purpose and acceptance would still remain, but comprehension of God's role as provider would not come naturally. This left mankind feeling very "needy," bringing tremendous motivation to find their own solutions apart from God. However, anything less than God would be a counterfeit, incapable of true fulfillment and satisfaction. Adam and Eve were not very good at distinguishing the difference, and neither are we.

How the Curse Affected Women

The curse interfered with Eve's need for acceptance. Moments before Eve left the Garden, God lovingly explained how the curse would play itself out.

> *Unto the woman he said, I will greatly multiply thy sorrow and thy conception; in sorrow thou shalt bring forth children and thy desire will be for thy husband.*
>
> *Genesis 3:16 KJV*

1. **Because of sin, women would now experience heightened anxieties.** Even though the word "sorrow" appears twice in this text, they are not the same words in the Hebrew. "Sorrow," as it first appears, means "worrisome"; it refers to emotional unrest. Women were designed to process life emotionally, bringing sensitivity to her husband's practical approach to things. But when sin entered the picture, her emotional makeup now included a reservoir of anxious thoughts that she could not resolve easily. She would fret about change, about relationships, and about the future. Fear would replace her joy, and soon she would begin to doubt God's love. Additionally, women would worry about conceiving; the very gift that distinguished them as female would no longer come with guarantees. For many generations, a woman's value was determined by her ability to conceive—especially sons. (This is still true in many countries of the western world.) Women were held responsible for infertility and suffered incredible misfortune, including abandonment and possible prostitution in order to survive.
2. **Because of sin, women would experience painful childbirth.** The blessing of new life passing from the womb into the world now included intense pain. "Sorrow" as it appears the second time in this text, is translated "toil, earthen vessel, pang, labor". This is a description of the physical pain women would experience in delivering a child. Eve was the perpetrator of their sin; she was deceived by the serpent. The Bible explains that painful childbirth is a form of redemptive suffering, reminding women of the price of sin and the provision of mercy (1 Timothy 2:15).

HOW THE CURSE AFFECTED WOMEN

3. **Because of sin, women would crave man's approval.** God also warned Eve that she would struggle with her role as a woman. *"Your desire will be for your husband, and he will rule over you"* (Genesis 3:16). Originally, men and women regarded one another as equal. Eve had just as much access to God and just as much value—she simply had a different purpose than that of a man. Eve was Adam's helpmate—her purpose being to assist him in serving God, but positionally she was not inferior to him in any way. None of that changed, even when they were expelled from the Garden, but Eve's ability to maintain confidence in her position was strained.

Adam struggled in other areas under the curse, but his masculine makeup somehow enabled him to maintain his identity with God. He did not strive to feel worth or acceptance. Eve, on the other hand, agonized over a feeling of loss. Even though her value never changed in God's eyes, the effects of the curse fragmented her ability to receive messages of God's love. Confidence gave way to doubt, leaving her with a desperate need for affirmation. Though God remained her true source for purpose, acceptance, and significance, the desire to feel value from a tangible source led her to seek the approval of men. In this sense, men would rule over her, not by God's design, but by an unmet need that brings a woman into submission of man's opinion of her.

The Curse Still Holds Women Captive

Even today, we observe how the curse still holds women captive. Women struggle to prove their worth and are easily persuaded to accommodate the lusts of men. This is a pitiful replacement for the

God of unconditional love but every girl is tempted to measure her worth by what men think. At a young age, little girls learn that part of being feminine means to look pretty. This God-given desire for beauty, however, takes on a destructive turn during impressionable teen years as girls become focused on their appearance, trying to measure up to an unwritten standard of perfection. Whether it's her weight, bra size, complexion, or hair texture, every young woman feels that she is deficient in one way or another.

Deceived by the demonic lie that her value depends upon appearance rather than character or faith, women face the pressure for approval. It is unavoidable. Sometimes a woman's only resolve for this tension comes in the form of destructive behavior. Anorexia, bulimia, cutting, and sexual promiscuity offer deceptive promises to relieve the tormenting messages of being unacceptable. Sadly, many women don't realize there is an alternative to be found in Christ's love.

Most recently, there has been a decline in modest dress, encouraging attention based on lust rather than respect. Tight clothing and cleavage is the fashion, but the message it sends completely discards dignity and respect. Women utterly despise being relegated to objects. No little girl ever grows up with a dream to become a *Playboy* centerfold, but the curse draws women into the clutches of such degrading practices because of their extreme thirst for approval.

Endless effort to gain the approval of a father, a husband, a pastor, or a boss only gives women temporary reward. God is our only true source of worth, but most women don't know the way back into His arms.

Eventually, some women grow weary of the "game" with its labyrinth of unwritten rules and they exchange their femininity for hostility—liberation from men. Exhausted from their efforts and wounded by their sacrifices, these "liberated" women have

HOW THE CURSE AFFECTED WOMEN

accumulated so much deep-seated resentment toward men that they reject all of them, claiming that men are lust-filled womanizers who are not necessary to society. They may blame men for their pain, but the true agony in their souls goes back to the Garden scene. Jesus is the only answer for their truest need.

Chapter 21

How the Curse Affected Men

Adam faced another version of the curse that targeted his critical need for purpose. Purpose gives meaning to life, and it is the essence of man's motivation to excel. Adam had a clear purpose, and it completely satisfied his desire for challenge and adventure.

> *"The Lord God took the man and put him in the Garden of Eden to work it and take care of it."*
>
> Genesis 2:15

Life in Eden came with an automatic management position. The Garden was quite vast, stretching over the territory of modern day Iraq in the beautiful river valley between the Tigris and Euphrates (Genesis 2:10–14). I'm sure it kept him quite busy. But that wasn't all. God gave Adam the job of naming all the animals (Genesis 2:19). This must have been an adventure! Can you imagine taking a safari ride with God? Work was a big part of life in Eden, but God made sure it was fun, loaded with the fulfillment of satisfying labor that included a reward for the effort. But sin changed all that, and God became far less accommodating. The curse affected Adam in three primary areas—pressure, frustration, and mundane tasks.

To Adam he said . . . "Cursed is the ground because of you; through painful toil you will eat of it all the days of your life. It will produce thorns and thistles for you and you will eat the plants of the field. By the sweat of the your brow you will eat your food, until you return to the ground, since from it you were taken; for dust you are and to dust you will return."

Genesis 3: 17–19 NIV

1. **Because of sin, Adam struggled with an intense fear of failure.** "Cursed is the ground because of you; through painful toil you will eat of it all the days of your life" (Genesis 3:17). The land represented Adam's vocation—the center of his accomplishments. In order to survive, he had to assume the role of primary provider for the family, and it came with the pressure to provide food, lodging, and protection for his family. Before the Fall, this was all provided by God. Eden had been more like a rain forest of well-established vegetation where abundant fruits and vegetables grew with relative ease. Now Adam's primary source of livelihood depended upon his own resources. It was a painful task that came with inescapable fears. The weather brought drought, the earth contained rocks (remember he had to make his own shovel), infections came with open wounds, and predators nibbled on the harvest, not to mention tyrannosaurus rex—yes, he was there(!). The future took on a foreboding feeling for Adam because the curse brought conditions that made success very difficult.

HOW THE CURSE AFFECTED MEN

2. **Because of his sin, Adam experienced frustrated efforts in order to provide for his family.** *"It will produce thorns and thistles for you."* (Genesis 3:18). Most likely, Adam didn't know a dandelion from a leaf of lettuce; remember, he had never had to weed a garden. But now he was faced with a much more difficult task of farming from the earth. The curse continually frustrated his efforts. *"And you will* (now) *eat from the plants of the field* (as opposed to the fruits of the trees)." While living in the Garden, God had provided an abundant supply of healthy, tasty vegetation that Adam and Eve didn't have to work for. All that had changed. Adam now had to build his own tools, clear a field, and plant a crop. It was a frustrating task that came with many excuses for anger—especially when all that work produced a patch of briars.

3. **Because of sin, Adam was unable to avoid expending energy for a mundane purpose.** *"By the sweat of your brow you will eat your food until you return to the ground, since from it you were taken; for dust you are and to dust you will return"* (Genesis 3:19). With hungry bellies, a growing family, crops to harvest, and hostile animals to dissuade, Adam didn't have much time left for fun. This must have been the thing he missed the most about Eden. It would be a *long* time before he'd have any neighbors to "hang out" with, so the absence of God's presence must have been very obvious. Work, sleep, work, sleep . . . the endless routine consumed his new life. It was a mundane existence that came with penetrating regrets.

These areas of struggle fed Adam's longing for greater purpose in his life to such a degree that independence from God became a continual temptation.

The Curse Still Tempts Men to Neglect God

The curse still leads men to believe that they have no valuable purpose in life; this area of weakness gives way to a myriad of man-made solutions. One extreme involves men who have abandoned their homes altogether because they don't want to face accompanying pressures and frustrations. The other extreme includes men who can't find time for home because the fear of boredom keeps them running at a marathon pace. Every man finds his place in this struggle to contend with the curse somewhere within the wide gap between the two poles.

John Eldredge, author of *Wild at Heart,* identifies three qualities of a man: the thirst to live an adventure, the determination to fight a battle, and the desire to win a beauty.[2] The curse discourages these instincts in a man. Every job has the thorns and thistles of discouragement and frustrated effort. Learning to navigate around those "joy-robbing" obstacles is labor-intensive, presenting men with unavoidable battles that are fought for a much less nobler cause. The fear of boredom fosters driven behavior and workaholic tendencies that replace balance. Moreover, the beauty he seeks is not impressed with convenient love. So stressful is the slavish lifestyle he chose that families suffer under the strain, leaving men blindsided by the tragedy of their neglect. Many men are apparently unaware that the satisfaction they seek can only be found in God's calling on their lives. The abundant life He offers to men not only includes purpose but balance, making room for variety, rest, and spontaneous fun.

The Road to Intimacy

Things have not changed much since the Garden. True satisfaction still depends upon the choice to walk in unity with God and one another. But the curse *does not* have to be an obstacle! Christ died to deliver us from the oppression of a cursed existence. He has given us power over a defeated outlook. Liberation from the curse mentality begins with learning to view our differences as God's tool to perfect His nature within us. Thankfully, men and women are not affected by the curse in the same ways. Because the two genders deal with life differently, this can be a platform for healthy growth. By appreciating those differences, men and women can learn from and contribute to one another. Relationships are then empowered by selflessness and sacrifice rather than fantasy romances, and God can use their respective strengths to meet one another's needs.

When our focus becomes what we can give rather than what we need, the love of God becomes tangible, and **"the way we were"** design is gradually realized. The way we are *is not* the way we have to stay.

Chapter 22

Love Is Sex—True or False?

We live in such a sexually saturated culture. Everywhere we turn, there are messages specifically designed to create arousal, leaving people with the distinct impression that sex is synonymous with love. Since everyone needs love, everyone must need sex—*as much as you can get, right?* If God gave us a free will and we each have a need for love, why can't we choose the lifestyle that best suits us? Why is God so narrow-minded about sex? Well, let's first consider how God defines love.

What Is Love, Anyway?

First Corinthians 13 describes what love should look like in a relationship. The apostle Paul wrote this eloquent text in a letter to Christians who were living in a culture that was very similar to ours today. It is a plumb line of righteousness for those seeking the truth about love. Tucked in the middle of the text is a little verse with a lot of meaning. "Love does not delight in evil, but rejoices with the truth" (1 Corinthians 13:6). Of course, love doesn't have anything to do with evil, but why did Paul waste the ink writing something so obvious? Because evil is based on deception; when someone is deceived, they don't realize they're wrong.

Today, there is evidence of every kind of evil, but deception regarding sexual love, in particular, leads many people to exchange the goodness of God for a lie. We have learned to "delight in" (or willingly participate in) evil because we don't recognize sin for what it is. With the prevalence of immorality in society, sinful practices are considered acceptable, and the definition of love soon becomes tainted with unrighteous visual images.

"What has been will be again, what has been done will be done again; there is nothing new under the sun" (Ecclesiastes 1:9). Sin is sin, but when it comes to sexual immorality, the Bible places this area of disobedience in a different category altogether. All sin negatively influences one's personal relationship with God, but sexual immorality infects an entire culture with its deadly influence, bringing destruction to large masses of humanity through disease and extermination of the unborn. Perverse mindsets also usher in powerful forces that turn nations away from viewing God in the context of goodness.

Tolerance Leads to Acceptance

By far, sexual sin is the greatest threat to eternal security because it leads people directly into the clutches of increasing deception. When you don't understand the value of God's Word, you won't be motivated to obey it. Those who have not formulated moral absolutes based on biblical truth are willing to tolerate practices that are contrary to God's plan. Eventually, tolerance leads to acceptance, and acceptance can lead to participation. Romans 1, clearly shows that God withdraws His convicting influence from those who practice sexual sin. Here's how it works.

A casual regard for righteous standards makes you vulnerable to popular, worldly mindsets. As a result, sinful preferences are developed that pollute your reasoning ability. Eventually, you'll move on to greater levels of deception and the reality of your need is hardly recognizable. Walking close to sin numbs your senses to the internal radar God has put within you to keep you from danger. You grow deaf to His voice of conviction and the blinking lights of "caution" in your spirit become dim. Convincing messages of compromise make it nearly impossible to discern truth from lie. The apostle Paul describes the gradual downfall of the Christians in Rome, sadly mentioning that God *gave them over* to the lifestyle of sin. Eventually, their lives no longer represented a testimony of Christ's influence because they were absorbed into the worldly system that rejects God.

Sex Should Be Loving

First Corinthians 13 defines love as an action that "***always protects, always** trusts, **always** hopes, **always** perseveres.*" Always is *all* ways—even sexually. If love equals sex, then the act should *always* be filled with the benefits of selfless commitment, respected confidences, the anticipation of future joy, and ultimate faithfulness. Sexual love is one form of love, designed for two married partners. Any sex outside this guideline falls into the category of sin. Sin *cannot* produce love because God does not exist in sin. You can lust for someone, and you can develop strong feelings for another human being, but ultimate love is only found in a relationship that's blessed by God. And God can't bless sin.

The Freedom to Choose

Amazingly, God gave us a free will to choose how to live. The apostle Paul declares, "*'Everything is permissible for me'—but not everything is beneficial*" (1 Corinthians 6:12). The freedom to sin is permissible. People engage in sin all the time, thinking that it's a harmless benefit of free will.

But what's *permissible* does not guarantee that it is *beneficial*. God cares too much about our destiny to let us live without standards of holiness. The nature of God's love is such that He could not place man in the Garden with the free will to choose without an owner's manual. *"My people are destroyed from lack of knowledge"* (Hosea 4:6), so God steps in to teach us how to survive and be successful.

True love recognizes ignorance and rises to meet the need. A mother, for example, doesn't let her baby play in the street because she's fully aware that the child cannot survive without her "laws," and she would be accused of negligence otherwise. Likewise, without God-given standards, life would be nothing more than endless attempts to figure out how we were created to function. With the strong influence of evil, men and women would eventually self-destruct: *"You, my brothers, were called to be free. But do not use your freedom to indulge the sinful nature; rather, serve one another in love. The entire law is summed up in a single command: 'Love your neighbor as yourself.' If you keep on biting and devouring each other, watch out or you will be destroyed by each other"* (Galatians. 5:13–15).

Ironically, true freedom is found by following the standards of righteous living that God outlines for us in the Genesis account. *"For the LORD God is a sun and shield; the LORD bestows favor and honor;* **no good thing does he withhold** *from those whose walk is blameless"* (Psalm 84:11). "Blameless" means those who avoid deliberate sin and/or unconfessed sin. It may come as a surprise, but God *really* does want you to enjoy life. He doesn't set up rules to keep you from having fun; they are established to help you avoid destruction and to lead you to greatness. *"But the man who looks intently into the perfect law that gives freedom, and continues to do this, not forgetting what he has heard, but doing it—he will be blessed in what he does"* (James 1:25).

LOVE IS SEX—TRUE OR FALSE?

Intimacy is what we all long for, but immorality is never the means to true love. It may offer pleasure, but sin is completely incapable of delivering the satisfaction found in intimate love. God did not design sex to be the source of human love. Sex is definitely an expression of love, but He never meant for anyone in His creation to fulfill our need for love. Sex becomes an idol when people depend upon it for self-esteem, worth, and significance. God doesn't like *anything* competing for His place in our lives. He alone is sufficient to satisfy *all* of our love needs. God designed sex for marriage. Within the boundaries of this relationship where a lifetime commitment of unconditional love is secure, sex has the right place. And God's design makes unlimited satisfaction possible.

Chapter 23

What's So Bad About Sin, Anyway?

Even if you're not a Catholic, the scene is familiar. A man with a guilty face pulls back the dark curtain to take a seat in the cubicle marked "Confessional." A darkened screen separates him from the priest who listens on the other side in a plush booth. "Bless me, Father, for I have sinned," he begins.

What's so bad about sin, anyway? We all know what sin makes us feel like, but is guilt the only way to recognize it? The Bible has much to say on the subject. Let's not jump too fast to a list of do's and don'ts. Saying hundreds of Hail Marys might ease your conscience, but it won't do much for purging your soul. The only way to get rid of the guilt is to hate sin, and the only way to do that is to understand what it is and what it does to people.

Sin Is Rebellion

It was not as if God hadn't made Himself clear. Adam and Eve both understood God's instruction. They were not to eat any fruit that grew on the Tree of the Knowledge of Good and Evil. They could choose from any other tree in the garden except for that one, but the couple made a deliberate decision to disobey God. So what? Plenty of people rebel against known standards. They even delight in the challenge of seeing how far they can go without being caught. Isn't rebellion another form of childish innocence? Not exactly. Rebellion positions you outside of God's field of blessing, unprotected from the enemy of your soul.

In the previous chapter, we established that God's laws are ultimately for our good; they keep us within the boundaries of righteousness, where prosperity and blessing are attainable. God's laws are not about keeping us *from* pleasure. Rather, they guide us *toward* goodness, which is far more satisfying. That is not to say that sin isn't sin when we don't understand that our actions are wrong. Even when we don't know the laws of God, we are still responsible for our actions, and our disobedience will affect us in a negative way.

Sin Is Enticing

Sin has a powerful influence over people because it is so deceptive. With persuasive words, sin offers false assurances that look very promising on the surface. This enticing message both flatters the flesh and minimizes the cost. Invitations come with the false guarantee of "better than" for everyone who consents. Notice Eve's reasoning for eating the fruit from the forbidden tree. *"When the woman saw that the fruit of the tree was **good for food** and **pleasing to the eye**, and also **desirable for gaining wisdom**, she took some and ate it"* (Genesis 3:6). Again, it wasn't that she had misunderstood God and didn't realize that the fruit was harmful. Sinful temptation caused her to rationalize disobedience. After concluding that there were actual benefits to eating the fruit, Eve completely disregarded God's instruction. The power of deception lures people away from righteousness with convincing fantasy.

Sin has a way of focusing on a need you have not been able to satisfy. The temptation will comment on your condition, communicating subtle messages that are shy of the truth. On the surface, these lies appear logical. Gradually, they gain the power to influence your will until a moment of desperation snowballs into a choice to sin, even when there is obvious harm and destruction in the offer.

Sin manages to convince people to do *anything but* righteous acts because sin is directly opposed to God. Ravenous temptations attempt to sway the hearts of men *away from* God. By far, the greatest strength of deception comes from making sin popular.

Sin *loves* company. Consider Eve's immediate action after she tasted the fruit—she offered it to Adam. There is power in numbers, and when a crowd of people agree to sin, deception has ultimate control. No matter how destructive or dangerous the sinful behavior is, temptation can convince you to join in the "fun" by using peer pressure. Pleasure may well be the bait, but the ultimate objective of sin is controlling many people at once. Once sin has the green light of consent, it has the power to persuade people to walk away from their beliefs and convictions. It all starts with the "everyone's doing it" message, a persuasive exaggeration that appeals to those striving for acceptance.

Sin Is a Trap

Since no man knows the future, who can tell him what is to come? No man has power over the wind to contain it; so no one has power over the day of his death. As no one is discharged in time of war, **so wickedness will not release those who practice it.**

Ecclesiastes 8:7–8

To take the bait, you have to enter the cage. You might think people would be smart enough to avoid the obvious, but the persuasive power of temptation entices them to swallow the bait without any consideration of the trapdoor locking behind them. With every disobedient choice, sin gains an advantage. While deception does the dirty work of convincing you that you're still in charge, the power of sin steadily influences your decisions. Sometimes it takes people years of sinful living before they realize that they can't willfully lift the latch and walk away scot-free. Their destructive lifestyle becomes a slippery slope of regrettable choices they can no longer control. Sin locks the prison door and throws away the key.

Sin is also a cruel warden that torments its victims. Much worse than Cinderella's stepmother, this prison guard will not only demand your service but will also delight in your suffering. We call it spiritual bondage. Bound by the power of lies, the victim is tormented by his captor with incessant accusations that pronounce guilt and condemnation. There is *no* reprieve! As a result, he is unable to regain self-respect, making him exceptionally vulnerable to lies that state he's unlovable and unredeemable. Hopelessness gives way to anger, and the sin cycle continues with an increasing capability to wound greater numbers of people. Sin holds the evidence to validate the lie, so the pit of depression, oppression, and remorse offers no escape whatsoever.

Sin Is Death

The apostle Paul says that *"the wages of sin is death"* (Romans 6:23). Wages are payment—the earnings from a transaction. When you agree to sin, you contract with death! Adam and Eve found out that sin's terms guarantee an exchange of suffering. Even though they did not die at that moment, their idea of living changed drastically. Not only did their sin begin the countdown to eventual physical death, but it also caused their cursed existence on earth. Death was now given permission to inflict pain, sickness, disease, drought, floods, and accidents—just to name a few—upon the beloved of God. Physical death included mourning, emotional death included depression, and spiritual death included hell.

Without a doubt, death is the power behind sin. Death uses temptation to lure people to rebel against God's righteous standards for the expressed purpose of swallowing up the souls of men. Many people are completely oblivious to the traps that are set because they don't believe sin is dangerous.

"There is a way that seems right to a man, but in the end it leads to death" (Proverbs 16:25).

Jesus used a parable about a farmer planting seeds to explain men's choices to His disciples (Luke 8:4–15). By far, the road most traveled is a broad path that represents the system of the world—a mentality not altogether consistent with Scripture, but one that appears "right" because many other people are walking down this road. However, Jesus said, *"The seed is the word of God. Those along the path are the ones who hear, and then the devil comes and takes away the word from their hearts, so that they may not believe and be saved"* (Luke 8:11–12). The broad path is within Satan's jurisdiction where he has the power to influence people away from the truth. A lifestyle of sin and indifference will lead them straight into the mouth of hell. *Sin is a rebellious decision, inspired by a powerful enticement that leads to a death trap!*

Good News!

The good news is that this destiny is totally preventable. Christ offers an alternative that comes with a full benefit package of blessings, but you gotta choose the way of holiness. It begins with a simple confession. "I'm sorry, Lord." Admit your sin. God will not turn you away. "I have a lot of regrets. I don't want to sin, but I do. Help me change." Make it your prayer and God will come near. I promise!

Chapter 24

Promiscuity . . . I Want To Be Accepted

There's a neighborhood in our area with beautiful new homes, each exuding an expensive appearance of charm. The American dream never looked so "homey" with landscaped front yards sending a variety of welcome messages. Surely, they are inhabited by a husband and wife, three kids, and a dog who all love each other, but this is not the case. The adults in this neighborhood have discovered a new form of entertainment—wife-swapping. It's adultery with consent, and even though they work to avoid that tiny, nagging voice of guilt, they've bought into the lie that sexual "freedom" is thrilling. In today's society, promiscuity has not only become prevalent but acceptable; God's plan for goodness has been replaced with a cheap rendition of fun. Remember, *sin is a rebellious decision, inspired by a powerful enticement that leads you to a death trap.*

Sex Was Never Intended To Be the Primary Focus

Sex was never intended to be our primary focus, but it has become the center of attention because it is a qualifying standard of acceptability. Sex is incapable of meeting our need for love; it was never created for that purpose. Yet, many people are caught in the trap of sexual promiscuity, believing that this lifestyle is "normal." Today, God's precious gift of virginity is sold for less than pennies at a slave auction. The new owners are spiritual wardens who are thrilled by the prospects of a new mind to torment.

No matter how glamorously the media portrays sex, *no one* can receive God's blessing when they are not following His guidelines. Most of what you see modeled on the screen is a counterfeit that conveys a lifestyle based on sin outside the righteous boundaries God set up for abundant living. The apostle Paul warns, *"Flee from sexual immorality. All other sins a man commits are outside his body, but he who sins sexually, sins against his own body"* (1 Corinthians 6:18). "Flee" is a very strong word that means "to escape, or to run away from something dangerous," and the Greek translation even adds "to shun." That kind of response to sin doesn't come unless you are convinced of its danger. You need to understand what sexual promiscuity does to you.

One Partner, Strongest Bond

How does someone *"sin against his own body"* when he or she has sex outside of marriage? First of all, sexual union is what the Bible calls "one flesh." It was designed by God to create a lasting bond between two partners, physically, emotionally, mentally, and spiritually. It is the one act that stands out from the rest because it also involves the soul, and it is strongest when two virgins remain sexually faithful to one another for a lifetime.

When you think about a piece of Scotch tape, it is the most adherent when it has only been used once. With every successive use, the tape loses its ability to stick to a surface and eventually cannot bond at all. This is a perfect analogy of what happens to you emotionally when you have multiple sexual partners. The result is a fragmented soul that is incapable of bonding to a spouse yet desperate for wholeness.

This point is even substantiated in recent studies of two biochemicals: oxytocin and vasopressin. Oxytocin has been nicknamed the "bonding hormone" because it is naturally produced in a woman during delivery and breast feeding to enhance bonding with the infant. But it is also produced in a woman during intercourse. Likewise, vasopressin is a produced in males during arousal, having similar bonding effects. "Chemicals released during intercourse, such as oxytocin and vasopressin, introduce a unique effect that promotes a series of pair-bonding behaviors. The primary exposure of the system to these chemicals seems to trigger a response that permanently alters body chemistry, and consequently behavior tendencies, making the individual (animal or human) more receptive toward his or her partner. Once the bonds are established, the disruption of these bonds causes great distress. It is clear that the body favors the maintenance of these bonds and reacts unfavorably when they are broken. Such data seem to show that the biochemistry of the body associated with sexual union is optimally designed to be experienced within the context of an intimate and permanent relationship."[3]

Every Partner Makes a Memory

Second, God created sex as a powerful expression of love between a man and a woman joined by a marriage covenant. It is designed for repetitious pleasure, completely dependent on the building blocks of private learning experiences. This pleasure is *only* found in the confines of monogamy where alternative sexual partners are completely denied.

Your memory is the greatest sex organ God has given you to stimulate healthy sexual response. When someone has sex outside of marriage, they open themselves up to memories that are totally unavoidable.

Practice *does not* make perfect when it comes to multiple partners! Both positive and negative experiences are lodged in a permanent memory bank, and they bring devastation to a marriage. Unavoidable comparisons to former partners, painful scenarios of rejection, and preconceived expectations strain the marriage relationship with intolerable, traumatic pain.

Promiscuity Is Habit Forming

Third, promiscuity perpetuates more sin. It is habit-forming and carries with it the indelible trademark of disease and death. Promiscuous behavior fosters a sexual preference for multiple experiences with a variety of partners. That desire does not stop when you become married. The habitual practice of sexual sin has already been established, and the marriage bed will be viewed as a boring alternative that cannot compete with promiscuous indulgence. This fleshly lifestyle is also plagued by sexual diseases that can cause painful intercourse, sterility, and miscarriages. Abortion often becomes the solution for unplanned pregnancies.

The Price of Acceptance

Sadly, the underlying motivation for sexual promiscuity is acceptance. Remember the Garden of Eden? Remember how God took care of Adam and Eve's need for acceptance? Everyone has a need to feel like they belong and are wanted—it's a key ingredient to intimacy. But God never intended for sex to be the price for acceptance. Sex was created to be a reward not a bargaining chip. You are accepted by God. You are loved by God. You are desirable, chosen, and preferred by a God who is crazy about you. Don't settle for anything less!

Chapter 25

Cohabitation . . . I Want To Be Sure

Hank is a college coach, and I direct a marriage ministry, so we get invited to a lot of weddings. I remember one in particular. Bill and Sally were so in love. He was quite the Prince Charming, treating her with protective care that never smothered. The look in his eyes told you he adored her. Sally was a bubbly young adult with a natural glow. Without reservation she communicated total admiration and devotion for Bill. They were truly made for love so they decided to live together. Bill came from a divorced home, and it motivated him to take the cautious route—he wanted to be sure this was a love that would last. Eventually, they decided to get married.

The wedding was absolutely magical. I remember her coming into the sanctuary through a side entrance. The moment she approached the center aisle their eyes met from across the room, and they both began to cry. It was a good thing she didn't wear makeup because they used more tissues than camera film.

Everyone loves to see two young people with a promising future of happiness—it restores the hope that love still works. But tragically, this one didn't. After ten years of marriage and two babies, Bill and Sally got divorced. What happened?

Divorce Proofing

Dr. Neil Clark Warren, author of *Finding the Love of Your Life* and founder of e-Harmony.com, a highly successful online dating service, reports that nearly 70 percent of Americans have experienced divorce on some level, either through a personal failed marriage or having been raised in a home with divorced parents.[4] No one could have anticipated the vast repercussions of this social epidemic that would generate such a dramatic shift away from traditional marriage. Having experienced the pain of divorce, many children are now growing into adulthood with the mistaken impression that traditional marriage just doesn't work like it used to. Rather than repeating the painful cycle, they are far more interested in finding an alternative to divorce.

Characteristically revolutionary, young adults conclude that the best prevention plan is to determine compatibility by living together. Before tying the knot they arrange a mock marriage, sort of like a "30-day trial or your money back" marketing strategy. Believing that they've got nothing to lose, the sexual benefits and financial independence are very inviting incentives with this lifestyle choice.

Today, the majority of never-married, young couples are waiting until their mid twenties for their wedding day,[5] but they're not waiting to "play house." One study from the University of Michigan determined that 50 percent of marriages in the last decade were preceded by cohabitation,[6] setting new trends for the premarriage lifestyle. But marriage isn't always the goal. Less than half of cohabitating couples have definite plans for marriage,[7] suggesting that fewer couples are interested in a long term relationships. Why? Because cohabitation is one way to divorce proof a relationship. If you're not married, you can't get divorced! But no one tells them that the strategy is a scam. Cohabitation is one of the best ways to end up in the Canyon of Love Failure.

Does Cohabitation Really Work?

Family life in America has been steadily changing since the 1960s, with cohabitation as the point man for new structure on the home front.[8] As a result, researchers have gathered a surplus of valuable data on unmarried couples who live together. Does cohabitation really work? Does it qualify as a healthy form of relating?

While people embrace the belief that cohabitation increases the likelihood of a successful relationship, statistics prove otherwise. The University of Michigan study also found that one sixth of couples living together last a minimum of three years together and only one tenth make it to five years. About 55 percent of cohabitating couples eventually marry, but only 40 percent make it to their five year anniversary.[9] Drunkenness, adultery, and drug abuse are the top three reasons for their failures.[10]

Social scientists William Axinn and Arland Thornton studied possible reasons for the high divorce rates among couples who cohabit prior to marriage. Does divorce occur by chance—the unfortunate mismatch of two singles who thought they were compatible? Or is there a predictable cause and effect to these repetitive circumstances? Their findings were unsettling. "Our analyses show that non-marital cohabiting relationships indeed are selective of those who are least committed to marriage and most accepting of divorce."[11] People who hesitate with a lifetime commitment tend to gravitate toward others who share their caution and it sets the course for a relationship that is temporary, at best.

Domestic abuse is also more common.[12] Without an established network of relatives and friends, there is less accountability and connectedness. Cohabitation is underscored by an incentive for independence, so expectations are often met with resistance. Because the relationship is not based on a commitment of unconditional love, selflessness, and sacrifice, cohabitation cannot support these critical virtues. Boundaries are difficult to establish, and violence is often used as the means to enforce one's "rights."

The most surprising findings, however, involve the overall satisfaction with relationships. The National Institute of Mental Health reported a higher rate of depression among cohabitating women in comparison with those who are married.[13] These women are also more prone to anxiety, specifically regarding the stability of the relationship. Sexual faithfulness is not supported by a vow of chastity. Consequently, multiple adulterous affairs with various partners go along with this kind of lifestyle, creating an environment of doubt, mistrust, and emotional pain.

And lastly, despite the imagery of young, cohabiting college students, most live-in arrangements include children.[14] Forty percent of homes with unmarried adults sharing a bed also share a house with kids. That means thousands of children are born to couples who are not preparing for parenthood. An unexpected addition to the "family" doesn't translate as exciting news, and decisions regarding the future are typically made hastily. These factors set the stage for incredible stress and dysfunctional responses arise—including child abuse. One study conducted at the University of Iowa found that 84 percent of the child abuse cases occurred in a single parent home, of which, 64 percent were committed by the mothers' boyfriends.[15] Perhaps the most ironic finding, however, is that the trend of divorce continues. Dr. Neil Clark Warren reports that "75 percent of all children born to cohabiting parents will experience their parents' separation before they reach age 16."[16]

Even though the lifestyle appears sensible, the true effects of this sin cannot be underestimated. God hates sin because of what it does to you, and cohabitation is no exception. Sexual relationships outside of marriage will steer you away from God's goodness. Remember, *sin is a rebellious decision, inspired by a powerful enticement that leads you to a trap of death.*

Chapter 26

Homosexuality . . . I Want To Be Real

In recent years, homosexuality has become increasingly accepted as a viable alternative lifestyle. Cultural trends have shifted traditional gender roles to make room for this small population, and strong voices of influence send convincing messages that homosexuals are victims of discrimination. As a result, many same-sex partners are finding it easier to "come out of the closet" in a society that is increasingly sympathetic to their lifestyle choice. Public approval has released homosexuals to live out their true identities—to be real. Their cause appears very liberating, but does sex really define who you are?

We have a family friend who recently determined that he was gay. He's young, but knowing Chris, this was not an impulsive decision. Taking on a new image is risky—a reputation could make or break you. But for Chris it was a moment of final concession, almost as if he was saying, "All right, I have these sensations, I might as well accept the fact that I'm gay." But after a year of pursuing a sexual relationship with his boyfriend and transferring most of his social life to homosexual circles, Chris made a profound comment, "No one wants to be gay. We all want to be straight, but we just have these feelings."

Sex is a behavior—one of many actions that contribute to our livelihood. But actions do not determine who we are. Thank goodness. I used to climb up on the kitchen counter to reach for the top shelf where

Mom kept the brown sugar. I would sneak a teaspoon even though I knew she wouldn't approve. But that did not make me a thief—at least not one for life. We have to answer for our actions, but it's a good thing we aren't defined by the accumulation of our behaviors. Forgiveness offers us the chance to change behavior, to get a fresh start. You don't really know the joy of living until you've been forgiven. Behavior is not permanent; change is possible.

I wonder about homosexuals who are living the lifestyle, convinced that they were born this way. "I just want to be real," they say. "This is the way I am so I might as well accept it," and they take up the cause, completely convinced that there is no alternative apart from sexual frustration. Surrounding approval validates their new identity as normal and safe, but I wonder how many of them really feel like Chris? Deep down they long for heterosexual impulses, but they resort to living a life of concessions. It's so far from true joy, and the price for adopting this identity is very high.

Self-Destruction

The homosexual lifestyle comes with a long list of dangerous health risks. Exposure to harmful bacteria and viruses is part of the sexual practice. Consequently, sexually transmitted diseases are prevalent. In 2002, the Center for Disease Control reported that MSM (men having sex with men) accounted for 93 percent of the syphilis cases in San Francisco and 81 percent in Los Angeles.[17] And in 2004 the CDC reported a 70 percent rise in syphilis cases nationwide, suggesting several sources that identify MSM as the primary contributors.[18] Venereal disease produces extreme pain, sterility, and susceptibility to HIV/AIDS and anal cancer. In 1997, five of the fifty states identified HIV/AIDS as the leading cause of death among men aged 25—44.[19] Current reports indicate that MSM accounted for an 8 percent rise in reported HIV/AIDS cases between 2003 and 2004, of which 70 percent of all male adults and male adolescents who received the diagnosis that year.[20] But death and sickness aren't the only ways homosexuals suffer. An HIV diagnosis also fosters a substantial number of mental illness symptoms. Anxiety disorders, major depression, and substance abuse occur much more frequently in same-sex populations.[21]

And the homosexual lifestyle includes unhealthy social standards. Promiscuity is a large part of the homosexual lifestyle. One study from the Netherlands—a country with a long history of gay communities—reports that steady homosexual relationships only last an average of 1.5 years, including up to eight casual partners outside the primary relationship a year.[22] "Sexual exclusivity among these couples is infrequent . . . Ninety-five percent of the couples have an arrangement whereby the partners may have sexual activity with others at some time under certain conditions."[23]

All of these factors contribute to a lifestyle that is self-destructive with life expectancies well below average. One study by the *International Journal of Epidemiology* reports that 42 percent of MSM (men having sex with men) will not reach their sixty-fifth birthday, and the majority of deaths range between ages 30 to 44.[24]

I wonder about people who willingly engage in sexual acts that are dangerous. How much energy is spent in denial, pretending that life is good? Who ministers to them when they're in pain or bleeding? Who comforts them when they attend yet another funeral? How do they resolve the fear of their own death? Change is possible, but somehow the message is not getting through.

The Voice of Reason

The apostle Paul said, *"Faith comes from hearing the message"* (Romans 10:17). God created our minds to generate a belief system based on what we hear, particularly repetitious messages. It's a powerful mechanism that can even sway public opinion, leading to trends that shape history. God gave you permission to choose what to believe. You can listen to society's voice of reason—it certainly is popular, but truth is far more than what looks and sounds right. Truth is based completely in the goodness of God's Word where His love for men and women is constantly repeated. And His *truth is always validated by consistent patterns of health, prosperity, and life for humanity.* When messages aren't based in the Bible, people unknowingly develop destructive opinions and beliefs. Health, prosperity, and life are no more lacking than in this lifestyle. For this reason, I believe God weeps for those who are trapped in the belief that life could never be different.

The Real You

Listen, men and women created by God, you are loved. I don't know your life story, but I do know that you are on a search for truth. You long to understand your design and your purpose. And God longs to tell you. He is your friend, the one and only who really understands who you are because He made you. He is a God who sustains life and makes it full of good things. He knows your dreams and desires. He knows what makes you smile, and He knows how to make you laugh. God is the only way to finding true joy and peace.

Change is possible, dear friend. Change is possible. Believe in the hope that life could be different, and God will show you the way of escape.

Chapter 27

Would You Like To Be Pure?

She was a woman who was full of sinful behavior. Her character had been permanently seared with a "scarlet letter" that earned her the red badge of reproach. No one felt sorry for her; after all, she had dug her own pit. She was friendless, and no one cared about her loneliness or her fears. She got what she deserved—she was "white trash," a whore that was used and wasted. Five men knew what it was to go to bed with her—at least the five she had called her husband. With that kind of reputation, there must have been countless others. The woman from Samaria had a lot of reasons to feel shame, but she wasn't necessarily in touch with the reality of her need.

No one cared if she lived or died. No one cared—but Jesus.

Do You Really Want To Be Free?

Jesus cares about your sinful condition so much that He is willing to take a detour through your hometown for the sole purpose of meeting with you just to prove it. That doesn't necessarily mean you'll receive what He has to say, however. The truth is what will set you free, but what if you don't feel shame? What if the truth is that you enjoy sin and don't really want to give it up? What if repentance is little more than head knowledge—a religious act that is more of an "ought to" rather than a "want to"?

You're eager for the relief of guilt, but a decision to completely abandon the sin is still on hold. What if the prospect of parting with sin is really scary for you? What if there is too much fear associated with change? What if you can't imagine life without the temporary comfort that sin brings? How can you ever find the courage to separate from the enticing trap that looks more like a party than a prison? How do you find the way into the light? How can you find your way to the cross?

Two walls of defense must be penetrated before the redemptive work of Christ can become real—the cultural bias and the courage to believe.

The Cultural Bias

Cultural bias sucks you into the flow of established norms, so the courage to consider life beyond those definitions is very hard to muster. Consider the Samaritan woman. She had *a lot* of reasons to completely blow Jesus off that day—excuses that were shaped by the culture in which she lived. The history of Samaria is one of contrasting loyalties. They were counted among the native Israelites, but they separated themselves from the laws of Moses by adapting the practices of false religions. Consequently, temple prostitution and human sacrifices became acceptable. The introduction of idolatry had such a powerful allure that it gradually led them down the path of self-destruction. Second Kings 6:26–29 describes a deplorable scene of cannibalism!

In light of their immoral reputation and new pagan rites, the Samaritans were an extreme embarrassment—a huge black eye for those who followed the Law of Moses with a clear conscience. Orthodox Jews deeply resented the rebellion of their ancestors and did not want to be associated with them. Their disdain was passed down through the generations, escalating to a form of racism.

The Samaritan woman's astonished comment to Jesus after He asked her for a drink is an example of the cultural rift: *"How can you ask me for a drink?"* (John 4:9) can be interpreted as "Jews don't eat from the dishes that Samaritans use." The cultural bias of that day did not allow for any provision of kindness between the two. Since the expected norm was hate, nothing within her sphere of experience could have prepared her for the exchange she had with Jesus that day. But she had come to draw water anyway.

Maybe your worldview excludes the notion of a merciful Jesus—your past didn't leave you with inviting impressions about the guy. In fact, perhaps not much of your childhood included any mention of Jesus at all. You may not have been raised in a home where going to church was a priority, and even if it was, the church setting may not have been a positive experience for you. Perhaps your family wasn't really a family. Interaction centered more on survival skills than relationship skills, and most of the adults in your life didn't enjoy the role of mentoring you. Maybe you were raised in a home with mixed messages: "The daddy who loves me is also the daddy who hurts me, rejects me, or never has time for me," or "The mommy who loves me also loves different men, but we don't live with my daddy." Maybe the most influential person in your life really wasn't a person but a television—a guide to answer your questions that were never verbalized. The TV taught you how to define what was "normal" by three particular guidelines: (1) requests are always made through sexual expression; (2) religion is boring, but spiritualism is exciting; and (3) Christians are ignorant hypocrites who cannot be trusted. When a society shapes your view of truth, even outrageous acts of sin become acceptable—that's how deception works.

Whatever your experiences, *nothing* about your worldview has ever introduced you to a God of gracious kindness and mercy. Like the Samaritan woman, you don't have any good reason to walk up to the well where a strange man sits. But if you're ever going to find true peace and joy, you're going to have to take a step of faith beyond the cultural bias of today.

Daring to Believe

I don't know how she mustered the courage to approach Jesus that day. There must have been something to distinguish Him as a Jew—perhaps his clothing—but her experience with this side of the family tree had been anything but positive. She was also a woman, so interaction with a man in public was forbidden, much less a private conversation with one. But her greatest obstacle was probably her reputation.

Commentators have speculated that she came to the well at the "sixth hour" (probably noon) to avoid people. Women came to the well in the early morning before the sun got hot. It was not only a time to start the chores, but it also served as the place of fellowship, where friendships were fostered amidst local gossip. The Samaritan woman intentionally planned her day to avoid their insults.

Bible scholars have also conjectured that her sinful behavior was not her choice. Women were often divorced because they were barren. Remarriage was permitted, but it was usually an arrangement of little more status than a concubine, with the expressed purpose of reproducing more sons. Her subsequent remarriages would suggest infertility, so she was quickly rejected. Women in this position were truly desperate. Without a welfare system, they were often forced into prostitution just to survive. The woman of Samaria had many reasons to hide that day, but she dared to believe that maybe there was a measure of mercy yet to be found.

To find your way to experience the goodness of God, you must dare to believe that He is a loving God. In your mind, there might be a hundred reasons why you should run away from God and not even give Him the time of day. But you'll have to develop more than a passing interest in His character before you can enjoy His goodness. I know "love" may only be little more than a four-letter word to you, but you'll have to cultivate a curiosity that's more than a passing thought. You'll have to look at the crucifix and dare to believe that it's more than just a gold-stained religious figurine hanging on the wall. You'll have to consider that just maybe Jesus did what He did because of love. Perhaps the depth of that kind of love is something you've *never* experienced before. The realization of a love deficiency must surface, and it has to become an itch that you can't scratch. When your curiosity becomes a quest to know that kind of love, you'll draw near to the well.

God's Acceptance

James 4:8 says, *"Come near to God and He will come near to you."* God shows up in the most ordinary of places, hoping to get your attention. Desperately wanting to be noticed, He'll intentionally cross your path just to meet up with you, but most of the time you won't recognize Him. All the woman of Samaria saw that day was a strange man she had never met dressed in a familiar outfit that didn't communicate friendship. Yet, there was something different about this person that drew her to His side. That "something" was love.

God radiates love like the warmth of a campfire on a crisp autumn night. Acceptance is the magnetic field that surrounds His presence, and no matter what you've done or where you've been, the force of His love overwhelms your shame in that very moment of meeting Him. His love brings indescribable peace—a gift that is freely given to you. But you still have one more wall to level before the love of God becomes a reality.

Chapter 28

Shame is the Thief of Intimacy

We were seated around a beautiful table having lunch at a women's conference. I don't remember anything about the speaker or the subject of her message, but some part of it must have addressed self-worth. What I do remember was a comment that my friend made. She described an exercise that she had participated in at another function in which they handed out small tile pieces of all shapes and colors. The instructions were to choose one tile piece from the box and to imagine it being a missing piece somewhere on the floor of a large home. My friend explained that they were then asked to personalize the tile piece and identify where they see themselves in the home. Some chose the tile floor of the foyer, which may have represented a friendly personality, while others selected the kitchen tiles to describe someone who enjoyed hospitality. My friend then turned to me and said with complete honesty, "I saw myself as the missing tile piece behind the toilet on the bathroom floor."

Shame Wounds Relationship

There are many reasons why people experience shame. It can involve a specific sin that was committed years ago—a regrettable decision made in a moment of weakness. Others tolerate an underlying guilty conscience, because they believe it is their penance. There are also those who struggle with the shame about sinful acts committed against them. Horrible experiences of rape, incest, and other forms of abuse can create prisons of the mind that control your perception of life. Regardless of the source, shame is a thief with a hidden agenda to pull you into the dark with a variety of fear-based defense tactics to keep you there. Shame wounds relationship because it shuts down any confidence that you are lovable. It keeps you hidden, removed from your true self, and incapable of fully contributing to relationships.

"Love your neighbor *as yourself.*" If you don't have love for yourself, if you don't even like yourself, there's no way to love your neighbor. Relationship involves a lot of trial and error. It is an ebb and flow of struggle and reward. When shame is a controlling influence, you don't have enough security to give to a relationship. The risk of pain is far too threatening. So people approach relationships with many emotional walls built to prevent pain. But intimacy isn't about managing a wall—it's about building a bridge. The only way to build a bridge is to get rid of the shame.

The Truth Will Set You Free

Jesus said, *"You will know the truth, and the truth will set you free"* (John 8:32). For me, truth was about being honest with myself—admitting the true motivations of my heart. Sometimes, the truth involves other people—things done in the private chamber of your mind or a shameful event you were forced to participate in. No matter what truth means to you, Jesus wants to set you free from the bondage of regret. He knows there is no peace in the prison of shame. Even though your sin is concealed, Jesus knows that you are not free. He loves you and wants to help you. He wants you to have free access to the abundant life that He died to give you, but you must make the choice to walk into the light to receive it.

The good news is that Jesus made a way to atone for our sin. That means He paid the debt for our sin so He could make a relationship with us possible. The hard news is that we have to walk into the light to get it. God *is* light, and there just isn't any other way to get to know Him without learning to like the light. For people who have lived within the dark caves of shame for most of their lives, it isn't easy to see God as inviting.

Shame Hates the Light

Light was *not* inviting to me! I had a huge issue with shame. I don't remember doing or saying anything in particular that might be classified as really shameful, but I definitely struggled with a guilty conscience. On the outside, I sure looked like I had it all together, but on the inside, I felt like I always fell short. I just didn't think I was acceptable. I had this nagging notion that everyone else could figure life out but me.

In my mind, I was deficient, so my remedy was to deny my true self and hide behind the locked door of shame. I started acting how I thought everyone else wanted me to act. As the years went by, I got quite good at it and eventually became sadly out of touch with who I really was. This did not make for an optimal marriage relationship. Weaknesses become obvious and the masks eventually fall off when you live with a spouse. I had spent so many years believing lies about myself that I couldn't express truth with confidence. This led to excruciating conversations that caused Hank's trust in me to wane. Shame resisted the light with a vengeance, and every attempt I made to be honest was met with a wave of guilt and uncertainty. I pictured myself in a beam of light that exposed my hideous condition, and I could hardly bear the sight. Without a doubt, I was the missing tile piece behind the toilet!

The experience was so painful that it forced me to be real, but my conclusion was not at all comforting—surely God would reject me. Many times over, I struggled with a great sense of doubt that God really loved me. The temptation to run back into hiding was strong, but I knew I needed to break through the stronghold that shame had over my mind. The only way to do it was to force myself to believe that God really wanted me.

What Does It Take?

What does it take to walk in the light? The Bible outlines for us one simple instruction: *"If we confess our sins, he is faithful and just to forgive us our sins and to cleanse us from all unrighteousness"* (1 John 1:9). Confession means admitting your guilt. It's saying, "I did it, and I'm sorry I did it." All God asks is that we confess our sin to Him with a heart of repentance and earnest remorse. This admission is what positions us in the light.

Even when you are forced to sin against your will, you have been exposed to unrighteousness. Rape and incest are horrific forms of abuse that foster deep wounds of guilt and shame. God doesn't blame you for the sin, but you are still in need of cleansing. In the Old Testament, people who had been exposed to a dead body were considered unclean. They had not been disobedient to the Law, but they had still handled something unclean. For this reason, they had to follow a ceremonial rite of cleansing to regain access to worship and the fellowship of other believers. Jesus longs to wash away all the shame associated with the sin. When you choose to be totally honest with God about your pain, healing can begin. "I hate that I was forced to sin, Lord. Please cleanse me and please heal me, God" might be a good prayer to help you start talking to God.

God also gives us another step that not only enables us to gain access into the path of light, but it also secures our position there.

"Therefore confess your sins to one another and pray for each other so that you may be healed."

James 5:16

When I first overcame the stronghold that shame had over my mind, I was still too weak to continually resist the temptation to return to my prison. Shame had been a life pattern that I had lived by for many years. I needed to confess my sin to a trusted friend who would hold me accountable to walking in the light of my true identity. I encourage you to find a spiritual leader you respect—one who can keep a confidence. Confess your sin to them, and let them help you develop a new life pattern based on the truth of God's love for you.

Chapter 29

Dating with a Purpose

She was a junior in high school with a desire to live for God. But none of her experiences with religion had prepared her for the mysteries of romance. Yeah, Jesus was her Savior, but He couldn't pass for a boyfriend! How did God fit into her love life? Deciding on the possibility that God must have a vague interest in this subject, she confided in Him for a prom date. Filled with hope for a fairy-tale journey, she trusted God to somehow make her high school dreams come true. She didn't really expect a knight in shining armor, but she wanted to be romanced. You know, just like they do in the "chick flicks." But somehow the list of respectable suitors was slim, and no one approached her with an invitation. She was pretty, popular, and fun—it just didn't make sense. But most of all she was thoroughly disappointed with God. *"I don't think I ask God for much, but right now I don't even think He knows my address."*

When It Comes to Dating, Is God Really Interested?

Have you ever felt that way? You truly desire to live for Christ but when it comes to dating, God simply says, "No comment." After all, how does a prom date request compare to a prayer for the war in Iraq? God and romance just don't mix. So you try to figure it out on your own. When you're single, you learn the unwritten social rules of dating by keen observation. To be somebody, you need somebody to notice you. You need someone of the opposite sex to find you attractive to show an interest in you. But when you uphold high standards of sexual purity, the list of available "somebodies" has definitely been shortened. In desperation, you try trusting God for direction, but the future is still full on unknowns and your social life is really boring. God's response seems so frustrating.

I want to encourage you. God is *definitely* interested in your love life. The modern singles scene may be far from fairy-tale romance, but God is totally amazed with your desire for love. He understands the challenges of living in a culture that's saturated in lust. He recognizes the intense desire to be found desirable, but He also knows about the confusing maze of mixed messages and the disguise of false love. Today's society approves what is harmful and selfish. The acceptable dating system is no longer framed by the social rules of etiquette. There are far too many casualties because of the absence of morals, and He wants to navigate you through the minefield of unnecessary pain. His desire is to see you enjoy every stage of this journey.

The Way It Used To Be

Christian dating used to come with a set of standards that every man and woman understood clearly. A guy would call and invite you to spend time with him. Usually it was to dinner, a ball game, or maybe a movie. He would pick you up, pay for the outing, and bring you home. All this happened with a mutual understanding that sexual exchange was not part of the date. And one date did not communicate an exclusive relationship. In fact, you could go on several dates with a variety of different people and that was completely acceptable. No one got hurt because this was how you got to know people of the opposite sex. Eventually, some determined that they really enjoyed each other enough to become exclusive, but that was not the norm. A group of friends spent a lot of time dating one another. It was really fun.

Romantic love should be contagious, and romantic love should be synonymous with God's goodness, but how does it work? How does God want me to handle relationships with the opposite sex? Let me answer that question with a question. What is the purpose of dating? What do you hope to gain from the experience? It should be a personal decision. We no longer live in a society governed by social etiquettes, so you can't wait around for it to happen. You have to decide what dating is and whether or not it is valuable to you.

How Can Dating Be Helpful?

I'd like to suggest several ways dating could be helpful to you:

1. ***It can help you develop social skills.*** Single people are extremely interested in the opposite sex, but they usually haven't had a lot of experience aside from a brother or sister. Men and women think and act very differently. Dating can bring you up close to a different gender without a large investment in the relationship.
2. ***It can help you learn self-control.*** Even without the sexual messages coming from our culture, sexual desire is at an all time high when you're young. We've already explained the good reasons to abstain before marriage, but it's still challenging to wait. Dating allows you to develop this skill. Self-control is essential to every healthy marriage, and it's best learned during the single years.
3. ***It can help you determine values.*** How you feel and what you feel about the issues of life are called values. As Christians, we know the Bible is our standard, but there are a lot of gray

areas in our society that don't fit into a neat package of right and wrong. Dating includes lots of communication that can help you determine righteous standards to live by.

4. ***It can help you choose a mate.*** Relationships are complex. There is a lot to sort through before you determine who you are and what draws you to or away from someone. Dating can help you determine intricate preferences that makes compatibility more obvious.

Dating should be purposeful—decide for yourself before you try it out.

Chapter 30

Dating Boundaries . . . Keeping Unnecessary Pain Out

You feel an attraction to someone, but you're not sure it's mutual. Are you the fool or the prize? God knows that romance is risky because learning to love means dying to self, and that always includes necessary pain. God wants to help you learn the art of love while avoiding *un*necessary pain. Dating is a perfect opportunity to build healthy relationship skills that can benefit you in the future. Given biblical guidance, dating can meet the desire for romance before marriage with a lot of clean fun.

Boundaries are the traffic lights that keep you on a moral path. They determine whether a relationship is safe to pass. You determine what the boundaries are—no one else can do that for you. But they should be private conclusions that come from lots of conversation with God.

Here are six tips that can help make dating a positive experience.

Tip #1: Learn to Keep Jesus as Your First Love

There is nothing better than the love of God. No relationship on earth can even compare to the satisfaction of knowing Jesus. I know you can't see Him face-to-face and gab over a cup of coffee, but God is definitely relational, and He wants to be number one in your life. So how do you keep that focus when you're exploring romance? You talk to Him about everything and anything. Include Him by simply asking for His advice. Talk to Him about your fears, desires, and dreams. He really wants to hear about what you're going through. The Wonderful Counselor is *very good* at listening and responding with affirmation, wisdom, and kindness.

Exploring romantic relationships can be very scary because you come close to sharing your heart with someone. It takes time to find someone you can trust with your heart. But when Christ is your love source, the one you rely on for approval, acceptance, and ultimate companionship, dating does not have to be so risky. Many young adults miss this important piece of relationship building and suffer enormous pain. When you make Jesus your first love, He will navigate you through the Canyon of Failed Love.

Tip #2: Learn the Value of Friendship

Friendship is a relationship apart from any romantic attraction. Without the pressure to impress, there's a lot of freedom in friendship. Whether male or female, a friend will accept you as you are. Your attitudes, moods swings, and "bad hair days" don't interfere with a true friendship because there is a measure of unconditional love defining the relationship. That's *exactly* why developing a friendship is so important in a dating relationship. The mutual attraction for another may come to an end, but when you take time to form a friendship, there is a foundation of respect that keeps the emotional investment from wounding your heart.

Many relationships are primarily based upon emotion, and the focus quickly shifts to doing the "couple thing." Public affection becomes the defining moment, but it's often inappropriate. We've all seen couples making out on the beach, pretending to be in love. True intimacy, however, begins with friendship, in which physical relations are kept at a respectful distance. A focus on friendship *enhances* romance and preserves the soul. The classic sign that a couple is keeping a balance in this area is the time and attention they give to other friendships. When you are dating with a positive purpose, you will not abandon other friendships.

Tip #3: Learn to View Dating as a Lab

One of the biggest challenges in dating is getting around the distracting question, "Is *this* the one?" It's hard enough struggling to overcome your own curiosity, but there's usually not much relief on the home front either. Family and friends hint, predict, and conclude all kinds of things, but the purpose of dating is simply an opportunity to experiment with relationships. Mate selection is an important part of dating once emotional intimacy has been established with a special someone, but there's a lot to learn before you pick out a diamond.

Most people your age do not have well-defined values. They have a general idea of what is moral, but that doesn't necessarily mean it comprises a conviction. Values are the basis of standards that shape your decisions and focus for life. It takes time to sort and sift them out before you determine just what you think about any given issue. Dating gives you the perfect opportunity to discover your values.

There are so many different kinds of people to meet and learn from. Dating can be an open forum for mutual learning. When you're in a lab, you won't get it right every time. In fact, you'll make more mistakes than anything. The same is true with building relationships. Learning to be comfortable with your strengths and weaknesses is a necessary part of finding intimacy. Relax. No one would expect you to pass Romance 400 at the age of twenty-one. You have permission to practice when you view dating as a lab. You'll have a lot more fun on the journey to intimacy.

Tip #4: Learn To Be Up Front at the Beginning

I think the hardest part about dating is the fear of rejection. No one likes to be hurt by someone they once trusted. You can avoid this pain by simply being up-front about your intentions. On the first date, explain your desire to keep the relationship positive. You might say something like, "I really enjoy spending time with you, but I just want you to know that I'm not ready for a serious relationship. My feelings may tell me that I'm ready for more, but I've got a lot to learn before I can be entrusted with someone's heart."

From there, you can talk about what your dating relationship will mean. It's nice to have a partner at social events and someone to do things with. If it's an exclusive relationship, you may need to redefine "serious." Are you referring to getting engaged, or does it mean having a relationship that emphasizes physical intimacy? Someone who is worth your time and energy will appreciate your honesty and respect your desire to gradually develop a relationship.

Tip #5: Learn to Establish Physical Boundaries

Song of Solomon 2:7 says, *"Do not arouse or awaken love until it so desires."* God specifically designed sexual love for the marriage relationship, but how far is too far? How are you supposed to know your limits in a dating relationship? The answer is *self-control*. Many dating partners buy into today's lie that sex validates their love; however, self-control is the greatest expression of true love because it's selfless.

Sex is a powerful expression of love that God designated for the marriage bed alone, but your body will not naturally abstain until marriage. Your body was created for sexual arousal whether you're married or not, but hormones are not a license to sin. It takes measurable self-control to abide by God's directive or *boundary*.

God expects you to set up physical boundaries to keep your dating relationships celibate. You must ask Him to help you determine which actions cause emotions to be "aroused" in you. Then you must decide what you should do to prevent this arousal from happening. Self-control is a critical part of godly intimacy, and dating presents you with the opportunity to build this character trait as a discipline for life.

Tip #6: Learn to Identify Mentors

A mentor is someone who has a measurable influence on your life. When they speak, you listen. They are wonderful teachers who can model healthy relationships skills. If you don't have one, ask God to show you someone He has placed along your path to offer you guidance. It may be a parent, pastor, teacher, or friend, but one thing is for sure, they have the gift of wisdom. Just because someone cares about you and really wants the best for your life doesn't necessarily mean their advice is wise.

Mentors have been appointed by God to guide your path in righteousness by speaking the truth. They are aware of the prevailing call of God on your life that was evident before the dating season even began. When the emotions that go along with attraction are aroused, it's easy to lose sight of what God has deposited in your heart. Love can make you justify sin and compromise your convictions, but a good mentor will not hesitate to hold you to a righteous standard. If you really want to avoid unnecessary pain, ask them to hold you accountable. Listen to their warnings when they see you investing in a relationship that doesn't line up with God's plan or when you're showing signs of ungodly romance. Mentors will ask the tough questions about things done in private. Every couple should find one or two. Seek their counsel and submit to it.

Chapter 31

Finding Mr./Ms. Right

They sat next to each other without any obvious display of affection. He was a hog farmer who laughed at his own jokes. With a big heart for mankind, he managed to support his family through farming just to learn a skill that could be useful on the mission field. She was a housewife with simple dreams, an engaging personality, and a smile that ended every sentence. Her two passions included Jesus and family. She wasn't much of a housekeeper, but she could make a ham potato casserole to die for! With undeniable zeal for Christ, both of them led intelligent conversations on a variety of subjects, articulating biblical relevancy with ease. They were simply intriguing.

It was the first night of a couples' Bible study, and we introduced ourselves by answering one simple question: "What attracted you to your spouse?" When it was their turn to answer the question about the one thing that attracted them to each other, he responded without hesitation, "She could weld!"

Yes sir. Meeting in an agriculture class at the local community college, their eyes met over a flame. Compatibility was obvious, and marriage just made sense. Their practical approach to mate selection saved them a lot of trial and error in defining love. They were confident that emotions would come in time.

The Practical Approach

Have you ever thought about the practical side of finding Mr./Ms. Right? Too many couples base their relationship on feelings rather than wisdom. But God calls us to walk life with much more practical interest. Proverbs typifies wisdom in feminine terms. *"Do not forsake wisdom, and she will protect you; love her, and she will watch over you"* (Proverbs 4:6). Who doesn't want the security of a good decision, especially when it comes to mate selection? Wisdom, rather than emotions, will guide you along a protected path.

Let's take a look at some of the questions you should ask yourself before you pop the question.

1. ***Do you have similar callings or career plans?*** God has a destiny for every man and woman, but some of those plans work well together and some do not. If you know where you're heading, you will definitely want to choose someone who will support you far beyond casual agreement. "That's great, I hope you make it" will not carry you through the trials of that calling or career. You want to find a mate who believes in you and who is prepared to stand along side you through the entire journey, even if plans fail.
2. ***Do you have similar interests?*** If you're not sure of God's plan for your life, you should at least share common interests. What do you do in your downtime? Does the other person enjoy doing the same things? What do they spend their money on? Do they gravitate to the similar investments? Common interests make fun happen—a quality ingredient in every strong marriage.

3. **How do they spend their money?** Jesus said, *"Where your treasure is, there will your heart be also"* (Matthew 6:21). You can learn *a lot* about someone's priorities by how they spend their money. This will forecast probable marriage victories or struggles. Are they impulsive spenders? Do they save money? Do they tithe? Do they have debt, and are they paying it back?
4. **Do you have similar backgrounds?** Background heavily influences what a person prefers and values. Customs and expectations for marriage and family life are all shaped through ethnicity, socioeconomic status, and religious upbringing. The more you have in common, the less you have to readapt.
5. **What is their relationship history?** Have they already been married? Have they already been sexual? If so, do they have a STD? Are they willing to be tested? Have they experienced rejection or abuse? What is their relationship with their parents? All these questions are based in wisdom. You should know what a person has already experienced before you came on the scene because it will definitely surface in your relationship at some point.

I once worked with a young woman who was preparing for her wedding. Rather than a "hope for the best" perspective on married love, Monica embraced an exceptional focus of truth. Recalling a conversation she had with her bridesmaid who questioned how she knew Tony was the "right one," she responded without hesitation, "I don't. Personally I don't believe there is one 'right one,' and while you can know who is wrong for you, it's darn near impossible to say who is a 'perfect fit,' especially in a case like ours where we've only been in a relationship for six months. I don't care if he's 'the one'—he's the one I choose, and I am committed to that choice. Some might say there's no romance in that, but I beg to differ. The truth is that there's nothing genuine about the whole philosophy of fate, chance, and luck. Mysticism is an ephemeral adrenaline rush; but when you commit to unreservedly giving your all to someone else, something is produced that is eternal, tangible, and inexplicably the most fulfilling joy in the world."

The bottom line is—include God in your search for that special someone. There is no prototype for godly romance. His orchestrations cover a vast array of intriguing scenarios. But determine to fall in love with marriage as a destination. This is God's plan for intimacy, and it is well worth the effort.

Chapter 32

Intimacy Is God's Plan for Love

God's plan for married love is called intimacy, but it's far more than permission to finally make love. Intimacy is a description of the quality of love God intended to be shared by a husband and wife—a love filled with a beauty that far exceeds anything known on this earth. Married love is often expressed sexually, but it is not limited to or defined by a sensual exchange. Intimacy is an emotional bond of extraordinary oneness in which transparency finds a place of rest beyond the clutches of shame.

> *The man said, "This is now bone of my bones and flesh of my flesh; she shall be called 'woman' for she was taken out of man."*
>
> *For this reason a man will leave his father and mother and be united to his wife, and the two will become one flesh.*
>
> *The man and his wife were both naked and they felt no shame.*
>
> Genesis 2:23–25

When two people are joined in holy matrimony, they break away from parental control to establish a new union of two lives. The couple makes a vow before God and a public audience that they will love one another unconditionally for the rest of their lives. The vow is a plea of faith, because both partners trust in a love that has never been tested. The limitations of human love are not yet realized, but their trust is in the God of love who has promised to navigate them through the maze of married life. This trio—God, husband, and wife—journey through married life through a love affair that God calls intimacy.

There's No Love Without Commitment

Hank and I were married for twelve years before we understood the unconditional love of God and how it worked in our relationship. As devout Christians, we knew God played a big role in a marriage relationship, but the concept was vague. We knew much more about Christian culture than we did about walking in love, and it made for a weak relationship. Articulate in Christianese, active in church service, and bold in our witness, we were confident that our marriage and family were exempt from the divorce trap. We had no idea just how vulnerable we really were to the schemes of Satan. Our confidence was nothing more than hypocrisy, and the enemy found plenty of room to pillage our relationship. The strength of his strategy centered around indecision regarding our commitment to each other.

Because of Hank's abusive past, he had many fears still hidden in the recesses of his mind. The vivid memory of his mom hiding under the bed from his alcoholic father was one of many that traumatized his ability to be intimate with me. He didn't know how to trust another person who had the capacity to hurt him again. Even though it never came up in conversation, I knew that the back door was an option in his mind. He could leave the marriage before enduring another round of emotional pain. I tried to love him in spite of his negative expectations, but my love was woefully imperfect, deeply inadequate.

Unintentionally, I often triggered a painful memory that led to an angry confrontation. With many fears of my own, I learned how to lie in order to keep relative peace, but it set me up for a secret life I never let Hank share.

We were headed for the Canyon of Failed Love! Our marriage eventually reached a crisis stage, and divorce was a serious consideration. But God reminded us of our commitment—the vow we made before Him at the wedding altar on a June morning in 1984. "For better or for worse, till death do us part" is what we promised one another. Even though we couldn't see any spark of romance in our relationship at the time, we made the decision to fulfill our vows. This, in turn, gave God permission to begin teaching us about our individual needs. He was the only one qualified to fulfill the desperate longing of our hearts for perfect love, and we began to understand how to accept it by faith and walk in it by grace.

With renewed confidence in God's unfailing love for us personally, we found the strength to not only close the door of divorce but also cement the opening. Divorce will never again be a consideration in our relationship. Since that time, we've been on the journey toward intimacy. The love we share is deep and long—far beyond what we have ever experienced. I know now that we never could have experienced this level of intimate union apart from commitment.

The Fairy-Tale Influence

Have you ever noticed that, without exception, every fairy tale ends with the wedding proposal? The "happily ever after" *is* marriage! I couldn't agree more that marriage is the ultimate love experience, but the fairy-tale imagery is a stumbling block for many people. The entire story is a romantic build up to the wedding ceremony, leaving you with the impression that love just happens. Have you ever wondered how Cinderella's marriage turned out? She was raised in an abusive home filled with neglect and cruelty. Can you imagine the kind of struggles she faced in her marriage?

God didn't create the brain with a "delete" button. There's no way to live out your future apart from the influence of your past. Fiction, on the other hand, leads you to believe that marriage is a fairy-tale "fix-all" and that "happily ever after" comes without much effort. Let me share a piece of reality with you—married love takes a lot of work! Romance is not automatic or constant. Intimacy is *developed* through the seasons of life and brings more reality to love than your first kiss.

Intimacy Is Fashioned in the Fire

Intimacy is fashioned in the heat of trials. I know that doesn't sound very inviting, but pain is what makes love very special. That's exactly why you need commitment. *Nothing* else is strong enough to keep you from running away from pain! Regardless of your childhood experience, you have a certain affection for your parents. Even if you lived through an abusive relationship, you still manage to maintain a measure of loyalty to them in your adult life. That's because they are your mom and dad; everyone has two biological parents who gave us life. That fact alone assures a level of devotion, even in the face of neglect. But a spouse is someone you *choose* to love. You don't have a choice about who parents you, but you *do* make the decision of whom to marry. That distinguishes the love you have for parents from the love you have for a spouse. When that relationship is sealed with a lifetime commitment to love unconditionally, intimacy has a chance to grow.

Life is an ebb and flow of joy and trials. A married couple chooses to walk down every road together. There's no way to predict what kind of trials a couple will face, but God uses difficult seasons to solidify love. He uses trials to melt down the hearts of pride, independence, and stubborn will in order to strengthen a supernatural union He calls intimacy. It is an extraordinary bond that defines your love as unique and set apart from any other relationship. No matter how sensual the exchange or how strong the compatibility may be, you *cannot* produce the same quality of love that comes from walking through a painful time together. Let me share a piece of reality with you—married love takes a lot of work! Romance is not automatic or constant. Intimacy is *developed* through the seasons of life and brings more reality to love than your first kiss.

Intimacy Is Established in the Face of Truth

Typically, the nature of a trial has to do with your marriage and if it doesn't, then you can be sure that the struggle will eventually play out in your relationship. The death of child, the loss of a job, the flat tire on a hot day in July—the stress of these circumstances will bring out your weaknesses, and eventually you will let down your guard with your spouse. That's the way marriage is *supposed* to work! The real you is not very pretty, but you need to deal with those areas of weakness. It's not easy when your spouse becomes a mirror—you come face-to-face with the truth about your own sinful condition. But married life is God's way of exposing the truth without humiliation. It's an awesome plan, because it provides the perfect opportunity for people to face the flesh in privacy.

Many couples reach this painful juncture and falsely conclude that love never existed in the first place. Rather than face the truth, they choose divorce. But a critical piece of God's plan to build intimacy includes the tension brought about by conflict. The simple truth is that your words and actions caused pain. Pressing through the struggle to get to the truth, you begin to realize your contribution to the conflict. It has a direct connection to the same sinful nature that put Christ on the cross. Suddenly the authentic love of God has a chance to grow within this tender area of remorse. Unconditional love thrives in the power of forgiveness, and God's plan for marriage successfully establishes yet another depth of intimacy.

You can't find love in a romance novel or by living together because intimacy takes sacrifice, unconditional love, and commitment. True love is discovered in-between the average day-to-day routine of dirty socks, Little League, mortgage payments, emergency room visits, and graduation parties. Intimacy cannot be bought or bartered. It takes time—a lifetime, in fact, that's developed every day of every year. Like fine wine, intimacy is perfected with age.

Divine Intimacy Changes Human Relationship

God knew that humans could not find love on their own, so He sent His Son to model love unconditionally. God knew that man could not receive His Son on his own, so He proved His love through sacrifice. God also knew that humans could not enjoy His love on their own, so He sent His Spirit to remind us of His commitment to return for us. There is no one who loves more perfectly than God Himself, and He is eager to share that love with people. With God's love as a constant, you can pass the test of endurance and discover the art of intimacy. The world is longing to see the real thing.

Endnotes

[1] David Nephin, Associated Press Writer, "Woman Missing for 10 Years Says She Was Controlled by Older Man," *Gettysburg Times*, sec. A1, March 24, 2006.

[2] John Eldredge, *Wild at Heart: Discovering the Secret of a Man's Soul* (Nashville, TN: Nelson Books, 2001).

[3] Dianne S. Vadney, "And the Two Shall Become One: Biochemistry and the Theology of the Body," *Ethics and Medics* 30 (April 2005):1-4.

[4] Neil Clark Warren, *Finding the Love of Your Life* (Wheaton, IL: Tyndale House, 1992), 10.

[5] David Popenoe, "American Family Decline, 1960-1990: A Review and Appraisal," *Journal of Marriage and the Family* 55 (August 1993):527-542.

[6] Pamela J. Smock, "Cohabitation in the United States: An Appraisal of Research Themes, Findings, and Implications," *Annual Review of Sociology* 26, no. 1 (2000):1-20.

[7] Larry L. Bumpass and James A, Sweet, "The Role of Cohabitation in Declining Rates of Marriage," *Journal of Marriage and the Family* 53 (November 1991): 913-927.

[8] Larry L. Bumpass, "What's Happening to the Family? Interactions Between Demographic and Institutional Change," *Demography* 27 (November 1990):483-498.

[9] Smock, "Cohabitation in the United States," 3.

[10] Michael D. Newcomb and P. M. Bentler, "Assessment of Personality and Demographic Aspects of Cohabitation and Marital Success," *Journal of Personality Assessment* 44, no. 1 (1980):11-24.

[11] William G. Axinn and Arland Thornton, "The Relationship Between Cohabitation and Divorce: Selectivity or Casual Influence?" *Demography* 29 (August 1992):357-374.

[12] Kersti Yllo and Murray A. Straus, "Interpersonal Violence Among Married and Cohabiting Couples," *Family Relations* 30 (July 1981):339-347.

[13] Myrna M. Weissman and others, "Affective Disorders," in *Psychiatric Disorders in America: The Epidemiologic Catchment Area Study*, Lee N. Robins and Darrel A. Regier, eds. (Toronto: The Free Press, 1991), 71-73.

[14] Bumpass, "The Role of Cohabitation" 913-927.

[15] Leslie Margolin, "Child Abuse by Mothers' Boyfriends: Why the Overrepresentation," *Child Abuse and Neglect* 16 (1992): 541-551.

[16] Neil Clark Warren, "The Cohabitating Epidemic," *Focus on the Family Magazine* (June/July 2003): 10.

[17] CDC, "Trends in Primary and Secondary Syphilis and HIV Infections in Men Who Have Sex with Men – San Francisco and Los Angeles, 1998-2002," *MMWR* 53, no. 26. (July 9, 2004): 575-578, http://www.cdc.gov/mmwr/preview/mmwrhtml/mm5326a1.htm.

[18] CDC, "HIV/AIDS Among Men who Have Sex with Men [fact sheet]," (May 2007), http://www.cdc.gov/hiv/topics/msm/resources/factsheets/pdf/msm.pdf.

[19] Robert S. Hogg and others, "Modeling the Impact of HIV Disease on Mortality in Gay and Bisexual Men," *International Journal of Epidemiology* 26, no. 3 (1997):657-661.

[20] CDC, "HIV/AIDS Among Men," 1.

[21] R. Stall and others, "Association of Co-Occurring Psychosocial Health Problems and Increased Vulnerability to HIV/AIDS Among Urban Men who Have Sex with Men," *American Journal of Public Health* 93, no. 6 (2003):939-942.

²² Maria Xiridou and others, "The Contribution of Steady and Casual Partnerships to the Incidence of HIV Infection Among Homosexual Men in Amsterdam," *AIDS* 17, no. 7 (2003):1029-1038.

²³ David McWhirter and Andrew Mattison, *The Male Couple: How Relationships Develop* (Englewood Cliffs, New Jersey: Prentice-Hall, Inc, 1984), 252.

²⁴ Hogg, "Modeling the Impact of HIV Disease," 657-661. It references the statement, "One study by the International Journal of Epidemiology reports that 42% of MSM (men having sex with men) will not reach their 65th birthday and the majority of deaths range between ages 30 to 44."(citation 24) at the bottom of page 110.

About the Author

Cindy has worked on the ministry staff at Freedom Valley Worship Center in Gettysburg, PA as the Founder and Director of Rebuilders Marriage Ministry for nearly 10 years. She also worked as a pastoral counselor for Freedom Christian Counseling Service. After teaching Gettysburg Master's Commission three years ago, Cindy fell in love with young adults. She now spends most of her time teaching and writing on God's plan for love with a big heart for this generation. Drawing from principles based in the Song of Solomon, the author brings a unique approach to intimacy with a focus on the Bridegroom of Christ as the ultimate Lover. Her writings reflect years of "inner court" experiences with Jesus, helping people better relate to God's love and express it through relationship.

Finding Intimacy in a Love-Starved World is also available as a curriculum series. For more info please contact her by visiting her web site at www.rebuildersmarriageministry.org.

Cindy Janczyk
Rebuilders Marriage Ministry, Founder
Gettysburg, PA 17325

To Order This Book

For more information on how to order this book
or the curriculum series, write to:

**Cindy Janczyk
Freedom Valley Worship Center
3185 York Road
Gettysburg, PA 17325**

or visit:

www.rebuildersmarriageministry.org